Wisdom 365:

Daily Buddha and Daily Solomon

R. E. Sherman

ISBN-10: 1499113420
ISBN-13: 978-1499113426

Cover design by Katrina Johanson

Printed in the United States of America

Please visit our website: www.buddha-christ.info.
For information regarding author interviews, please call 541-821-4238.

CONTENTS

Forward

Oh, that we could all be wiser! If we were, surely we would be happier, life would be more meaningful and the world would be a better place. But how can we become more wise?

Why not pursue a daily diet of advice from two of the wisest men in history: Buddha and Solomon? 365 daily readings. This ground-breaking book provides a topically arranged collection of their terse, penetrating insights, presented side-by-side. Soak in their proverbs. Take them to heart. All it takes is a few minutes each day and you will embark on an uplifting journey. Become a seeker of wisdom. Here's an excerpt:

Solomon (950 BCE)

Do you see a man wise in his own eyes? There is more hope for a fool than for him.[1]

Buddha (525 BCE)

[63] The fool who knows his foolishness, is wise at least so far. But a fool who thinks himself wise, he is called a fool indeed.[2]

---

[1] Proverbs 26:12 (NASB).

[2] Friedrich Max Muller, trans., *The Dhammapada: A Collection of Verses, Being One of the Canonical Works of the Buddhists*, in vol. 10, Part 1, *The Sacred Books of the East*, translated by Various Oriental Scholars, edited by F. Max Muller, available at Dhammapada (Muller), Wikisource. All Dhammapada proverbs are from this source, unless otherwise noted.

ALL of Buddha's 423 proverbs appear in order. Right next to each of these proverbs is a similar one from Solomon or one of his contemporaries.[3] Brief comments conclude each day's reading.

Every day you will experience East meeting West, and your horizons will be broadened. Though they lived 400 years and 3,000 miles apart, the Buddha and Solomon often spoke in similar voices. Each reinforced and complemented what the other said.

---

[3] If the source is the Psalms, the quotation is either from King David, Solomon's father, or a contemporary, broadly defined, either of Kind David or Solomon. If from a contemporary, the source is not named, as they are typically anonymous. For a key to which translation of the Bible has been quoted, go to the References page at the end of the book.

Chapter One – The Twin Verses
(Days 1-15, Dhammapada 1-20)

Chapter One introduces the reader to basic truths about how our thoughts, speech and actions result in either good or bad situations, such as harboring hatred can result in violence, or living without self-control can result in a ravaged life.

Repeating grievances inflames animosity and hatred. Confusing truth for untruth can injure others and unravel our lives.

Seeking after knowledge and wisdom and exerting self-control can safeguard us from many troubles. Taking delight in doing good helps others and ourselves.

Day 1

Solomon (950 BCE)

For as he thinks within himself, so he is.[4]

The hope of the wicked [ends] only in wrath.[5]

The desire of the righteous ends only in good.[6]

Buddha (525 BCE)

[1] All that we are is the result of what we have thought: it is founded on our thoughts, it is made up of our thoughts.

If a man speaks or acts with an evil thought, pain follows him, as the wheel follows the foot of the ox that draws the carriage.

[2] If a man speaks or acts with a pure thought, happiness follows him, like a shadow that never leaves him.

What we focus on (either by thinking, hoping or desiring) has an enormous impact on who we become. Karma, both good and bad, is created not only by what we do but also by what is going on inside us. Our inner world determines the kind of person we are and will become.

---

[4] Proverbs 23:7a (NASB).
[5] Proverbs 11:23b, (NIV).
[6] Proverbs 12:20 (NIV).

Day 2

Solomon	**Buddha**
. . . He who repeats a matter separates friends. [7]	[3] "He abused me, he beat me, he defeated me, he robbed me,"—in those who harbour [*sic*] such thoughts hatred will never cease.
He who covers over an offense promotes love . . .[8]	[4] "He abused me, he beat me, he defeated me, he robbed me,"—in those who do not harbour [*sic*] such thoughts hatred will cease.

Repeating our grievances kindles and inflames whatever hatred we may have. Doing so can destroy even a strong friendship. It is far better to stop dwelling on harms inflicted on us by others, and to focus on positive thoughts or feelings instead. Best of all is to nurture loving attitudes.

---

[7] Proverbs 17:9b (NKJV).
[8] Proverbs 17:9a (NIV).

Day 3

Solomon   **Buddha**

Hatred stirs up strife, but love covers all transgressions.[9]

[5] For hatred does not cease by hatred at any time: hatred ceases by love, this is an old rule.

Acting on hate will not resolve or diminish our hatred. It only generates more conflict. The antidote for hate is to overcome it with love. Often, we can diffuse difficult situations with simple kindness, or a gentle reply.

Day 4

Solomon   **Buddha**

The wise man's eyes are in his head, but the fool walks in darkness. Yet I myself perceived that the same event [death] happens to them all.[10]

[6] The world does not know that we must all come to an end here;—but those who know it, their quarrels cease at once.

The sober fact is we all will die, the wise and the foolish alike. This knowledge ought to cause us to prudently consider our conduct in this life.

---

[9] Proverbs 10:12 (NASB).
[10] Ecclesiastes 2:14 (NKJV).

Day 5

Solomon

Buddha

The way of the sluggard is as a hedge of thorns; But the path of the upright is made a highway.[11]

Listen, my son, and be wise, and keep your heart on the right path. Do not join those who drink too much wine or gorge themselves on meat, for drunkards and gluttons become poor, and drowsiness clothes them in rags.[12]

[7] He who lives looking for pleasures only, his senses uncontrolled, immoderate in his food, idle, and weak, Mara (the tempter) will certainly overthrow him, as the wind throws down a weak tree.

If we are uncontrolled, immoderate, slothful, and are ruled by our sensual desires, we will face pitfalls in life, including poverty. Let us be self-controlled, moderate, industrious people who have their sensual desires in check. Then we will have fewer obstacles as we journey through life.

---

[11] Proverbs 15:19 (ASV).
[12] Proverbs 23:19-21 (NIV).

Day 6

Solomon	Buddha

Solomon

Prudence is a fountain of life to the prudent, but folly brings punishment to fools.[13]

In the house of the wise are stores of choice food and oil, but a foolish man devours all he has.[14]

Buddha

[8] He who lives without looking for pleasures, his senses well controlled, moderate in his food, faithful and strong, him Mara will certainly not overthrow, any more than the wind throws down a rocky mountain.

If we are wise and restrain ourselves, we are strengthened, and the evil one cannot overthrow us.

---

[13] Proverbs 16:22 (NIV).
[14] Proverbs 21:20 (NIV).

Day 7

Solomon

Buddha

Remove the dross from the silver, and out comes material for the silversmith.[15]

The LORD detests the thoughts of the wicked, but those of the pure are pleasing to him.[16]

Even a child is known by his deeds, whether what he does is pure and right.[17]

[9] He who wishes to put on the yellow dress without having cleansed himself from sin, who disregards temperance and truth, is unworthy of the yellow dress.

[10] But he who has cleansed himself from sin, is well grounded in all virtues, and regards also temperance and truth, he is indeed worthy of the yellow dress.

As a silversmith has to refine the silver before he can form it into its intended purpose, so we need to refine, cleanse, and purify our thoughts and actions in order to live a righteous, blessed life. Even as a child is known by their actions, so we are known by the way we conduct our lives. If we are not cleansed from sin, that sin will limit us.

---

[15] Proverbs 25:4 (NIV).
[16] Proverbs 15:26 (NIV).
[17] Proverbs 20:11 (NKJV).

Day 8

Solomon

Buddha

Wisdom will save you from the ways of wicked men, from men whose words are perverse, who leave the straight paths to walk in dark ways, who delight in doing wrong and rejoice in the perverseness of evil, whose paths are crooked and who are devious in their ways.[18]

Those also who render evil for good, they are my adversaries, because I follow what is good.[19]

Deceit is in the heart of those who devise evil, but counselors of peace have joy.[20]

[11] They who imagine truth in untruth, and see untruth in truth, never arrive at truth, but follow vain desires.

[12] They who know truth in truth, and untruth in untruth, arrive at truth, and follow true desires.

Obtaining and seeking truth, knowledge, wisdom, and understanding should be a high priority in our lives. Otherwise, we can confuse an untruth for truth. The wicked can deliberately portray an untruth as truth, in order to deceive those who are not grounded in truth and sway the ungrounded for their personal gain.

---

[18] Proverbs 2:12-15 (NIV).
[19] Psalm 38:20 (NKJV), a psalm of King David, Solomon's father.
[20] Proverbs 12:20 (NASB).

Day 9

Solomon

Buddha

Like a city whose walls are broken down is a man who lacks self-control.[21]

Receive my instruction in preference to [striving for] silver, and knowledge rather than choice gold, for skillful and godly Wisdom is better than rubies or pearls, and all the things that may be desired are not to be compared to it.[22]

The righteousness of the upright will deliver them, but the unfaithful will be caught by their lust [desires].[23]

[13] As rain breaks through an ill-thatched house, passion will break through an unreflecting mind.

[14] As rain does not break through a well-thatched house, passion will not break through a well-reflecting mind.

Knowledge, wisdom and self-control build a solid roof over our heads to keep us safe in times of trouble and are far more valuable than striving for monetary gain. Reflect and meditate on the truth. Cultivate wisdom and practice moderation.

---

[21] Proverbs 25:28 (NIV).
[22] Proverbs 8:10-11 (AMP).
[23] Proverbs 11:6 (NKJV).

Day 10

Solomon	Buddha
For I am about to fall, and my pain is ever with me. I confess my iniquity; I am troubled by my sin.[24]	[15] The evil-doer mourns in this world, and he mourns in the next; he mourns in both. He mourns and suffers when he sees the evil of his own work.
This is an evil in all that is done under the sun: that one thing happens to all. Truly the hearts of the sons of men are full of evil; madness is in their hearts while they live, and after that they go to the dead.[25]	

When we see the destructive nature of our sin, and we see the pain it causes to others and ourselves, we mourn and regret our actions. The madness of sin is a great burden we carry in this life and into the next.

---

[24] Psalm 38:17-18 (NIV), a psalm of King David, Solomon's father.
[25] Ecclesiastes 9:3 (NKJV).

Day 11

Solomon

Buddha

A man can do nothing better than to eat and drink and find satisfaction in his work. This too, I see, is from the hand of God.[26]

Every man also to whom God hath given riches and wealth, and hath given him power to eat thereof, and to take his portion, and to rejoice in his labor—this is the gift of God.[27]

[16] The virtuous man delights in this world, and he delights in the next; he delights in both. He delights and rejoices, when he sees the purity of his own work.

A virtuous, righteous man takes delight in the gift of work, in doing good work, and in the provision from it. Solomon saw rejoicing in and taking satisfaction from work as a gift from God, while Buddha expressed that the virtuous man takes delight in the purity of performing the work itself. Let us take delight in the work before us, and in working diligently.

---

[26] Ecclesiastes 2:24 (NIV).
[27] Ecclesiastes 5:19 (ASV).

Day 12

Solomon

For I am ready to fall, and my sorrow is continually before me. For I will declare my iniquity; I will be in anguish over my sin.[28]

But the wicked will be cut off from the land and the treacherous will be uprooted from it.[29]

The desire of the [consistently] righteous brings only good, but the expectation of the wicked brings wrath.[30]

Buddha

[17] The evil-doer suffers in this world, and he suffers in the next; he suffers in both. He suffers when he thinks of the evil he has done; he suffers more when going on the evil path.

Doing evil or committing sin causes anguish and suffering. It brings down trouble upon us (body, mind and soul) and others, and causes pain in this life and the next.

---

[28] Psalm 38:17-18 (NKJV), a psalm of King David, Solomon's father.
[29] Proverbs 2:22 (NASB).
[30] Proverbs 11:23 (AMP).

Day 13

Solomon

[Wisdom speaking:] Now therefore, listen to me, my children, for blessed are those who keep my ways. Hear instruction and be wise, and do not disdain it. Blessed is the man who listens to me, watching daily at my gates, waiting at the posts of my doors. For whoever finds me finds life, and obtains favor from the LORD.[31]

Blessed is the man [whose] . . . delight is in the law of the LORD, and in His law he meditates day and night. He shall be like a tree planted by the rivers of water, that brings forth its fruit in its season, whose leaf also shall not wither; and whatever he does shall prosper.[32]

Buddha

[18] The virtuous man is happy in this world, and he is happy in the next; he is happy in both. He is happy when he thinks of the good he has done; he is still more happy when going on the good path.

When we delight in the law and meditate on it, we are happy and blessed in this life and we flourish like a tree planted by a stream. Let us take joy in and think about the good we have done, then we are happy as we walk on the good path.

---

[31] Proverbs 8:32-35 (NIV).
[32] Psalm 1:1-3 (NKJV), a psalm of King David, Solomon's father.

Day 14

Solomon	Buddha

The wise in heart will receive commands, but a prating fool will fall.[33]

Wise people store up knowledge, but the mouth of the foolish is near destruction.[34]

[19] The thoughtless man, even if he can recite a large portion (of the law), but is not a doer of it, has no share in the priesthood, but is like a cowherd counting the cows of others.

Any prating fool can recite wise sayings or the law, without having it affect the way he conducts his life. We will be wise if we store up knowledge and meditate on it, receive commands and let them take root in our thoughts, and live accordingly. Forsaking hatred, let us embrace a mind filled with peace.

---

[33] Proverbs 10:8 (NKJV).
[34] Proverbs 10:14 (NKJV).

Day 15

Solomon	**Buddha**

Whoever loves instruction loves knowledge, but he who hates correction is stupid.[35]

The heart of him who has understanding seeks knowledge, but the mouth of fools feeds on foolishness.[36]

[20] The follower of the law, even if he can recite only a small portion (of the law), but, having forsaken passion and hatred and foolishness, possesses true knowledge and serenity of mind, he, caring for nothing in this world or that to come, has indeed a share in the priesthood.

Do we study just to be a know-it-all, to be puffed up with pride over how much we know, or do we love wisdom and knowledge? Are we humble in our efforts to learn? Do we apply what we learn? Our attitude is very important as we study.

---

[35] Proverbs 12:1 (NIV).
[36] Proverbs 15:14 (NIV).

R. E. Sherman

Chapter Two – On Earnestness
(Days 16-27, Dhammapada 21-32)

This chapter focuses on the importance of being earnest in our spiritual life. Being earnest is demonstrating a sincere, serious and determined intent in the quest for knowledge and wisdom, and in living out our values. The opposite is being thoughtless, careless, and even reckless in our choices.

Consistently seeking after wisdom will assist us in knowing what is important, what we ought to focus on, and what is of lasting value. The earnest seeker casts off vanity and pride and delights in meditating on the law (moral teachings).

Day 16

Solomon (950 BCE)

A kind man benefits himself, but a cruel man brings trouble on himself. The wicked man earns deceptive wages, but he who sows righteousness reaps a sure reward. The truly righteous man attains life, but he who pursues evil goes to his death.[37]

The lips of the [uncompromisingly] righteous feed and guide many, but fools die for want of understanding and heart.[38]

Do not be overly wicked, nor be foolish: why should you die before your time?[39]

Buddha (525 BCE)

[21] Earnestness is the path of immortality (Nirvana), thoughtlessness the path of death. Those who are in earnest do not die, those who are thoughtless are as if dead already.

Being earnest or serious in intention and effort, and being kind and living rightly benefits us. Being thoughtless, careless, even reckless and wicked leads us down a path of destruction and death.

---

[37] Proverbs 11:17–19 (NIV).
[38] Proverbs 10:21 (AMP).
[39] Ecclesiastes 7:17 (NKJV).

Day 17

Solomon

Buddha

A scoffer seeks Wisdom in vain [for his very attitude blinds and deafens him to it], but knowledge is easy to him who [being teachable] understands.[40]

The heart of him who has understanding seeks knowledge, but the mouth of fools feeds on foolishness.[41]

The heart of the discerning acquires knowledge; the ears of the wise seek it out.[42]

[22] Those who are advanced in earnestness, having understood this clearly, delight in earnestness, and rejoice in the knowledge of the Ariyas (the elect).

Understanding that wickedness leads to death, our earnest and discerning decision to seek wisdom and knowledge will lead us to a good and joyful path through life.

---

[40] Proverbs 14:6 (AMP).
[41] Proverbs 15:14 (NKJV).
[42] Proverbs 18:15 (NIV).

Day 18

Solomon

Buddha

By wisdom a house is built, and by understanding it is established; and by knowledge the rooms are filled with all precious and pleasant riches. A wise man is strong, and a man of knowledge increases power.[43]

Wisdom makes one wise man more powerful than ten rulers in a city.[44]

[23] These wise people, meditative, steady, always possessed of strong powers, attain to Nirvana, the highest happiness.

By wisdom and knowledge, we can build our lives and the result of that is being strong when tough times come, being powerful in a constructive manner, and ultimately being happy, because the wisdom and knowledge obtained, assists us in knowing what is important, what is of value, and what is worth focusing and meditating on.

---

[43] Proverbs 24:3-5 (NASB).
[44] Ecclesiastes 7:19 (NIV).

Day 19

Solomon

Buddha

Who may ascend the hill of the LORD? Who may stand in his holy place? He who has clean hands and a pure heart, who does not lift up his soul to an idol or swear by what is false.[45]

The thoughts of the wicked are shamefully vile and exceedingly offensive to the Lord, but the words of the pure are pleasing words to Him.[46]

[24] If an earnest person has roused himself, if he is not forgetful, if his deeds are pure, if he acts with consideration, if he restrains himself, and lives according to law,—then his glory will increase.

Purity in mind, heart, body and deed paves the way to becoming fulfilled.

---

[45] Psalm 24:3-4 (NIV), a psalm of King David, Solomon's father.
[46] Proverbs 15:26 (AMP).

Day 20

Solomon

Buddha

The righteous shall never be removed: but the wicked shall not inhabit the earth.[47]

The wicked are overthrown, and are not: but the house of the righteous shall stand.[48]

[25] By rousing himself, by earnestness, by restraint and control, the wise man may make for himself an island which no flood can overwhelm.

By evil thoughts and conduct, we bring down destruction upon ourselves. We will be overthrown. But by pure thinking and living, we inherently create a fortress (dike) of safety and blessing around our lives.

---

[47] Proverbs 10:30 (KJV).
[48] Proverbs 12:7 (KJV).

Day 21

Solomon

Buddha

How blessed is the man who finds wisdom and the man who gains understanding. For her profit is better than the profit of silver and her gain better than fine gold. She is more precious than jewels; and nothing you desire compares with her.[49]

A discerning man keeps wisdom in view, but a fool's eyes wander to the ends of the earth.[50]

[26] Fools follow after vanity, men of evil wisdom. The wise man keeps earnestness as his best jewel.

If we are foolish, vainly chasing after those things which flatter us and have no true value, we may wander to the ends of the earth doing so. If we are earnest and discerning, we keep wisdom as a treasured jewel, ever before us, guiding us on the best path.

---

[49] Proverbs 3:13-15 (NASB).
[50] Proverbs 17:24 (NIV).

Day 22

Solomon	Buddha
Lust not after her beauty in your heart, neither let her capture you with her eyelids. For on account of a harlot a man is brought to a piece of bread, and the adulteress stalks and snares [as with a hook] the precious life [of a man].[51]	[27] Follow not after vanity, nor after the enjoyment of love and lust! He who is earnest and meditative, obtains ample joy.
Oh, how I love your law! I meditate on it all day long.[52]	

It is far better to enjoy being earnest and meditative than lustful. Sensual pursuits, in particular those driving us to solicit prostitutes or participate in adulterous relationships, will lead to disastrous consequences: sapping our financial resources and possibly ending with the loss of life.

---

[51] Proverbs 6:25-26 (AMP).
[52] Psalm 119:97 (NIV).

Day 23

Solomon

Surely you desire truth in the inner parts; you teach me wisdom in the inmost place.

Create in me a pure heart, O God, and renew a steadfast spirit within me.[53]

Buddha

[28] When the learned man drives away vanity by earnestness, he, the wise, climbing the terraced heights of wisdom, looks down upon the fools, serene he looks upon the toiling crowd, as one that stands on a mountain looks down upon them that stand upon the plain.

Earnestly desiring a pure heart, seeking wisdom and having a steadfast and willing spirit, this will allow us to look upon others in kindness and compassion, with a desire to teach and share the good path.

---

[53] Psalm 51:6, 10 (NIV), a psalm of King David, Solomon's father.

Day 24

Solomon	**Buddha**
Do not correct a scoffer, lest he hate you; rebuke a wise man, and he will love you. Give instruction to a wise man, and he will be still wiser; teach a just man, and he will increase in learning.[54]	[29] Earnest among the thoughtless, awake among the sleepers, the wise man advances like a racer, leaving behind the hack.

If we respond to correction and instruction, and are alert and eager to learn, we will grow in wisdom. The foolish laugh and scoff at correction and instruction. Being thoughtless and asleep, they are left behind in the dust as the wise advance.

---

[54] Proverbs 9:8-9 (NKJV).

Day 25

Solomon

Buddha

Rescue those being led away to death; hold back those staggering toward slaughter. If you say, "But we knew nothing about this," does not he who weighs the heart perceive it? Does not he who guards your life know it? Will he not repay each person according to what he has done?[55]

[30] By earnestness did Maghavan (Indra) rise to the lordship of the gods. People praise earnestness; thoughtlessness is always blamed.

"But we knew nothing about this." As we journey through life, playing dumb or being thoughtless of our own behavior or of others can lead to great trouble in our lives. Once the truth comes to light, there can be a heavy price to pay, as it causes people to distrust or blame us. Better to be earnest and honored, than thoughtless and blamed.

---

[55] Proverbs 24:11–12 (NIV).

Day 26

Solomon	Buddha

It is the blessing of the LORD that makes rich, and He adds no sorrow to it. Doing wickedness is like sport to a fool, and so is wisdom to a man of understanding. What the wicked fears will come upon him, but the desire of the righteous will be granted. When the whirlwind passes, the wicked is no more, but the righteous has an everlasting foundation.[56]

[31] A Bhikshu (mendicant) who delights in earnestness, who looks with fear on thoughtlessness, moves about like fire, burning all his fetters, small or large.

It is foolish to delight in doing evil and to think of wickedness like a sport. When the storm comes, the wicked, foolish man is blown away because he has no foundation. If we are constantly eradicating evil thoughts and actions from our lives, refusing to be fettered by them, we will have a strong foundation.

---

[56] Proverbs 10:22-25 (NASB).

Day 27

Solomon

Buddha

For a righteous man may fall seven times and rise again, but the wicked shall fall by calamity.[57]

Pride goes before destruction, a haughty spirit before a fall.[58]

[32] A Bhikshu (mendicant) who delights in reflection, who looks with fear on thoughtlessness, cannot fall away (from his perfect state)—he is close upon Nirvana.

A malicious man disguises himself with his lips, but in his heart he harbors deceit. Though his speech is charming, do not believe him, for seven abominations fill his heart. His malice may be concealed by deception, but his wickedness will be exposed in the assembly. If a man digs a pit, he will fall into it; if a man rolls a stone, it will roll back on him.[59]

The illustration of rising or falling paints a vivid picture, but is also literal. If we delight in meditation on the law and avoid thoughtlessness and pride, we rise. If we allow pride and malicious attitudes to take root, we fall. After a minor fall, we can pick ourselves up and persist in doing good, but a major fall can cause great ruin our lives.

---

[57] Proverbs 24:16 (NKJV).
[58] Proverbs 16:18 (NIV).
[59] Proverbs 26:24-27 (NIV).

R. E. Sherman

Chapter Three – Thought

(Days 28-37, Dhammapada 33-43)

Our thought-life is examined in this chapter. The flighty mind runs wild, but the discerning man keeps wisdom and knowledge as paramount. Taming our minds is an ongoing task. Strengthening and training our minds through discipline is like building a fortress against temptation.

Receiving correction, instruction, and knowledge helps us achieve a well-directed mind. Consistent small corrections of our thoughts can keep us on the right path, like guiding a horse with small movements of the rider's hands.

Day 28

Solomon (950 BCE)

Discretion will guard you, understanding will watch over you.[60]

Take firm hold of instruction, do not let go; guard her, for she is your life.[61]

In the paths of the wicked lie thorns and snares, but he who guards his soul stays far from them.[62]

Buddha (525 BCE)

[33] As a fletcher makes straight his arrow, a wise man makes straight his trembling and unsteady thought, which is difficult to guard, difficult to hold back.

"He's a straight arrow" is a common description of someone who does the right thing consistently. Restraining or straightening out our thoughts and actions and doing the right thing can be difficult, but the reward is avoiding the thorns and snares of wickedness, which bring destructive forces upon us.

---

[60] Proverbs 2:11 (NASB).
[61] Proverbs 4:13 (AMP).
[62] Proverbs 22:5 (NIV).

Day 29

Solomon	**Buddha**

A wise man fears and departs from evil, but a fool rages and is self-confident.[63]

The highway of the upright turns aside from evil; he who guards his way preserves his life.[64]

[34] As a fish taken from his watery home and thrown on dry ground, our thought trembles all over in order to escape the dominion of Mara (the tempter).

When faced with evil, let us be wise and tremble with fear and depart from it immediately. This will protect our thoughts from temptation, and will guard us from harm, perhaps even saving our lives.

---

[63] Proverbs 14:16 (NKJV).
[64] Proverbs 16:17 (AMP).

Day 30

Solomon	**Buddha**

A discerning man keeps wisdom in view, but a fool's eyes wander to the ends of the earth.[65]

Above all else, guard your heart, for it is the wellspring of life.[66]

[35] It is good to tame the mind, which is difficult to hold in and flighty, rushing wherever it listeth; a tamed mind brings happiness.

[36] Let the wise man guard his thoughts, for they are difficult to perceive, very artful, and they rush wherever they list: thoughts well guarded bring happiness.

The flighty mind runs wild, but the discerning man keeps wisdom and knowledge as paramount. Taming our minds is an ongoing task. A well-guarded thought life brings happiness, and a well-guarded heart is a fountain of life.

---

[65] Proverbs 17:24 (NIV).
[66] Proverbs 4:23 (NIV).

Day 31

Solomon	**Buddha**

Righteousness guards the man of integrity, but wickedness overthrows the sinner.[67]

A discerning man keeps wisdom in view, but a fool's eyes wander to the ends of the earth.[68]

[37] Those who bridle their mind which travels far, moves about alone, is without a body, and hides in the chamber (of the heart), will be free from the bonds of Mara (the tempter).

Picture a strong horse being bridled and guided with the small movements of the rider's hands. Often small, consistent correction of our thinking can prevent great folly. To be able to discern right from wrong, to seek after wisdom and knowledge, to have integrity, if these are the guiding forces in our lives, we will be free from bondage to temptation.

---

[67] Proverbs 13:6 (NIV).
[68] Proverbs 17:24 (NIV).

Day 32

Solomon

Buddha

Where there is no revelation, the people cast off restraint; but happy is he who keeps the law.[69]

The law of his God is in his heart; his feet do not slip.[70]

[38] If a man's thoughts are unsteady, if he does not know the true law, if his peace of mind is troubled, his knowledge will never be perfect.

Knowing the true law and keeping it steadies the mind and keeps us from slipping into evil ways. Without understanding the law and disciplining the mind, there is nothing to restrain our wayward ways. We will be blessed and happy if we keep the law.

---

[69] Proverbs 29:18 (NKJV).
[70] Psalm 37:31 (NIV), a psalm of King David, Solomon's father.

Day 33

Solomon

Do not be overrighteous, neither be overwise—why destroy yourself? Do not be overwicked, and do not be a fool—why die before your time? It is good to grasp the one and not let go of the other. The man who fears God will avoid all extremes.[71]

Do not fret because of evildoers, nor be envious of the wicked; for there will be no prospect for the evil man; the lamp of the wicked will be put out.[72]

Buddha

[39] If a man's thoughts are not dissipated, if his mind is not perplexed, if he has ceased to think of good or evil, then there is no fear for him while he is watchful.

Moderation is key to avoid living a life of being excessively devoted to pleasure (dissipation) and the extremes of being overly righteous or overly wicked. In the end, there is no reason to fear the wicked, as they will be undone by their own actions.

---

[71] Ecclesiastes 7:16-18 (NIV).
[72] Proverbs 24:19–20 (NKJV).

Day 34

Solomon

Buddha

It is not good to have zeal without knowledge, nor to be hasty and miss the way.[73]

When the scoffer is punished, the simple is made wise; but when the wise is instructed, he receives knowledge.[74]

[40] Knowing that this body is (fragile) like a jar, and making this thought firm like a fortress, one should attack Mara (the tempter) with the weapon of knowledge, one should watch him when conquered, and should never rest.

Zealousness alone will not help us find our way. We should strengthen our minds like a fortress, and fill them with knowledge. We cannot assume that once a temptation is conquered that we can rest from our diligence. It is an ongoing task. We must be watchful.

[73] Proverbs 19:2 (NIV).
[74] Proverbs 21:11 (NKJV).

Day 35

Solomon

Buddha

As he had come naked from his mother's womb, so will he return as he came. He will take nothing from the fruit of his labor that he can carry in his hand.[75]

[41] Before long, alas! this body will lie on the earth, despised, without understanding, like a useless log.

All men die. This is a fact. We enter the world naked and depart in the same condition. We cannot take anything from our labors with us. Our bodies are just a shell, made from the dust of the earth, and after death are like a fallen log.

Day 36

Solomon

Buddha

Do not envy wicked men, do not desire their company; for their hearts plot violence, and their lips talk about making trouble. A wise man has great power, and a man of knowledge increases strength.[76]

[42] Whatever a hater may do to a hater, or an enemy to an enemy, a wrongly-directed mind will do us greater mischief.

A wrongly directed mind can do us greater harm than even one that hates deliberately. Don't envy the wicked or seek his company. A wise man has greater power, wisdom and knowledge. He is stronger than the wicked.

---

[75] Ecclesiastes 5:15 (NASB).
[76] Proverbs 24:1-2, 5 (NIV).

Day 37

Solomon

Buddha

He whose ear listens to the life-giving reproof will dwell among the wise. He who neglects discipline despises himself, but he who listens to reproof acquires understanding. The fear of the LORD is the instruction for wisdom, and before honor comes humility.[77]

Whoever loves instruction loves knowledge, but he who hates correction is stupid.[78]

[43] Not a mother, not a father will do so much, nor any other relative; a well-directed mind will do us greater service.

To achieve a well-directed mind, listen and receive correction, instruction and knowledge. Such a mind will be of greater service to you than the service any relative could render. Having a humble, teachable mind is the beginning of the journey to understanding and wisdom.

---

[77] Proverbs 15:31-33 (NASB).
[78] Proverbs 12:1 (NKJV).

Chapter Four – Flowers

(Days 38-49, Dhammapada 44-59)

The path of virtue is likened to a clever man finding the right flower. This chapter discusses ways of finding the virtuous path, such as listening to instruction, receiving knowledge, seeking wisdom, responding to correction, overcoming evil, and doing so with a humble heart.

Being aware of our frailty and the reality that we all will see death can keep us focused on walking a pure path. Living like a bee collecting nectar from flowers and doing them no harm, we ought to be diligent to live with integrity and not to harm others. Like the scent of a flower, our virtue ought to pervade those around us.

Day 38

Solomon (950 BCE)

Listen, my son, accept what I say, and the years of your life will be many. I guide you in the way of wisdom and lead you along straight paths. When you walk, your steps will not be hampered; when you run, you will not stumble.[79]

Buddha (525 BCE)

[44] Who shall overcome this earth, and the world of Yama (the lord of the departed), and the world of the gods? Who shall find out the plainly shown path of virtue, as a clever man finds out the (right) flower?

How do we find the way of wisdom and the path of virtue? If we listen to instruction, receive knowledge, seek wisdom, respond to correction and overcome evil, all with a humble heart, we will not be hampered, and we will not stumble.

---

[79] Proverbs 4:10-12 (NIV).

Day 39

Solomon

Buddha

Get wisdom, get understanding; do not forget my words or swerve from them. Do not forsake wisdom, and she will protect you; love her, and she will watch over you. Wisdom is supreme; therefore get wisdom. Though it cost all you have, get understanding.

The path of the righteous is like the first gleam of dawn, shining ever brighter till the full light of day. But the way of the wicked is like deep darkness; they do not know what makes them stumble.[80]

[45] The disciple will overcome the earth, and the world of Yama, and the world of the gods. The disciple will find out the plainly shown path of virtue, as a clever man finds out the (right) flower.

The wicked stumble in darkness. They are blind to their own folly. If we desire to be a disciple, we must seek wisdom, understanding, and the path of righteousness. We must overcome evil. Then our path through life will be like the first light of dawn, shining ever brighter.

---

[80] Proverbs 4:5-7, 18-19 (NIV).

Day 40

Solomon

Also they are afraid of height, and of terrors in the way; when the almond tree blossoms, the grasshopper is a burden, and desire fails. For man goes to his eternal home, and the mourners go about the streets. Remember your Creator before the silver cord is loosed, or the golden bowl is broken, or the pitcher shattered at the fountain, or the wheel broken at the well. Then the dust will return to the earth as it was, and the spirit will return to God who gave it.[81]

Buddha

[46] He who knows that this body is like froth, and has learnt that it is as unsubstantial as a mirage, will break the flower-pointed arrow of Mara, and never see the king of death.

Our bodies are like the froth in the ocean's waves, and we are like a mirage. We are made of dust and return to the earth as dust, but our spirits return to God and never see death.

---

[81] Ecclesiastes 12:5-7 (NKJV).

Day 41

Solomon

Buddha

The desire of the lazy [slothful] man kills him, for his hands refuse to labor. He covets greedily all day long, but the righteous gives and does not spare.[82]

[47] Death carries off a man who is gathering flowers and whose mind is distracted, as a flood carries off a sleeping village.

[48] Death subdues a man who is gathering flowers, and whose mind is distracted, before he is satiated in his pleasures.

Death carries the lazy, meandering man away as a flood destroying a sleeping town. He wastes his time and energy coveting rather than working. It is far better to work hard and share generously from our earnings.

---

[82] Proverbs 21:25–26 (NKJV).

Day 42

Solomon	Buddha
Do not say to your neighbor, "Come back later; I'll give it tomorrow"—when you now have it with you. Do not plot harm against your neighbor, who lives trustfully near you. Do not accuse a man for no reason—when he has done you no harm.[83]	[49] As the bee collects nectar and departs without injuring the flower, or its colour [sic] or scent, so let a sage dwell in his village.

We should not plan harm against our neighbor, or bring an accusation against anyone for no real reason. Like the bee who works diligently and causes no harm to the flowers, let us live with integrity, be generous, work diligently and live peaceably with our neighbors.

---

[83] Proverbs 3:28-30 (NIV).

Day 43

Solomon	**Buddha**

Solomon

A king who sits on the throne of judgment winnows out all evil [like chaff] with his eyes. Who can say, I have made my heart clean, I am pure from my sin? Diverse weights [one for buying and another for selling] and diverse measures—both of them are exceedingly offensive and abhorrent to the Lord. Even a child is known by his acts, whether [or not] what he does is pure and right.[84]

Buddha

[50] Not the perversities of others, not their sins of commission or omission, but his own misdeeds and negligences should a sage take notice of.

As a King sits in judgment of his people, so we ought to judge ourselves rather than focus on the failings of other. We ought not to favor ourselves by using a lighter or less severe measure as we judge ourselves.

---

[84] Proverbs 20:8-11 (AMP).

Day 44

Solomon	Buddha
The purposes of a man's heart are deep waters, but a man of understanding draws them out. Many a man claims to have unfailing love, but a faithful man who can find? The righteous man leads a blameless life; blessed are his children after him. When a king sits on his throne to judge, he winnows out all evil with his eyes. Who can say, "I have kept my heart pure; I am clean and without sin"? Differing weights and differing measures—the LORD detests them both. Even a child is known by his actions, by whether his conduct is pure and right.[85]	*[These both refer to Dhammapada 50: Not the perversities of others, not their sins of commission or omission, but his own misdeeds and negligences should a sage take notice of.]* [51] Like a beautiful flower, full of colour [*sic*], but without scent, are the fine but fruitless words of him who does not act accordingly. [52] But, like a beautiful flower, full of colour [*sic*] and full of scent, are the fine and fruitful words of him who acts accordingly.

Searching our own hearts for their purposes, winnowing out and repenting of our own misdeeds and failings, being a faithful, diligent person, having integrity (not using differing weights), seeking wisdom and knowledge to guide our ways, this is the life that is like a scented flower, full of color and fruitful.

---

[85] Proverbs 20:5-11 (NIV).

Day 45

Solomon

Buddha

I know that nothing is better for them than to rejoice, and to do good in their lives.[86]

[53] As many kinds of wreaths can be made from a heap of flowers, so many good things may be achieved by a mortal when once he is born.

Solomon tackled many great projects in his life. We too can follow the example of undertaking to do many good things in our lives, and yet not forgetting to keep wisdom and knowledge as a priority.

I undertook great projects: I built houses for myself and planted vineyards. I made gardens and parks and planted all kinds of fruit trees in them. I made reservoirs to water groves of flourishing trees. . . . I also owned more herds and flocks than anyone in Jerusalem before me. I amassed silver and gold for myself, and the treasure of kings and provinces. . . . I became greater by far than anyone in Jerusalem before me. In all this my wisdom stayed with me.[87]

---

[86] Ecclesiastes 3:12 (NKJV).
[87] Ecclesiastes 2:4-9 (NIV).

Day 46

Solomon

When it goes well with the
righteous, the city rejoices;
and when the wicked perish,
there is jubilation. By the
blessing of the upright the city
is exalted, but it is overthrown
by the mouth of the wicked.[88]

A wicked messenger falls into
trouble, but a faithful
ambassador brings health.[89]

Buddha

[54] The scent of flowers does
not travel against the wind,
nor (that of) sandal-wood,
or of Tagara and Mallika
flowers; but the odour [sic]
of good people travels even
against the wind; a good
man pervades every place.

Like the scent of flowers pervading a room, a good man affects all around him. When it goes well with him, the community rejoices. The wicked is overthrown by his own words and he perishes, and the community rejoices. Let us all be as a scented flower, a faithful ambassador of righteousness.

[88] Proverbs 11:10–11 (NKJV).
[89] Proverbs 13:17 (NKJV).

Day 47

Solomon

The righteous will flourish like a palm tree, they will grow like a cedar of Lebanon; planted in the house of the LORD, they will flourish in the courts of our God.[90]

But the path of the righteous is like the light of dawn, that shines brighter and brighter until the full day.[91]

He who trusts in his riches will fall, but the righteous will flourish like foliage.[92]

Buddha

[55] Sandal-wood or Tagara, a lotus-flower, or a Vassiki, among these sorts of perfumes, the perfume of virtue is unsurpassed.

[56] Mean is the scent that comes from Tagara and sandal-wood;—the perfume of those who possess virtue rises up to the gods as the highest.

The righteous will thrive like a green leaf, flourish like a palm tree, and grow like a cedar. Their path is like the bursting light of the dawn. The perfume of virtue is unparalleled and unsurpassed. Like the scent of a flower, it pervades those around it. Let us seek to walk the path of the righteous.

---

[90] Psalm 92:12-13 (NIV).
[91] Proverbs 4:18 (NASB).
[92] Proverbs 11:28 (NKJV).

Day 48

Solomon

Buddha

Righteousness (rightness and justice in every area and relation) guards him who is upright in the way, but wickedness plunges into sin and overthrows the sinner.[93]

[57] Of the people who possess these virtues, who live without thoughtlessness, and who are emancipated through true knowledge, Mara, the tempter, never finds the way.

We are emancipated through true knowledge, and can guard our way with thoughtful meditation on the law. Living with integrity, the tempter cannot overthrow us. Rightness and justice in every area of our lives, and in every relationship, guards us from destructive forces.

---

[93] Proverbs 13:6 (AMP).

Day 49

Solomon	**Buddha**
But the path of the [uncompromisingly] just and righteous is like the light of dawn, that shines more and more (brighter and clearer) until [it reaches its full strength and glory in] the perfect day [to be prepared]. The way of the wicked is like deep darkness; they do not know over what they stumble.[94]	58, 59. As on a heap of rubbish cast upon the highway the lily will grow full of sweet perfume and delight, thus the disciple of the truly enlightened Buddha shines forth by his knowledge among those who are like rubbish, among the people that walk in darkness.

The contrast of the righteous and the wicked, is like a flower growing up out of a rubbish heap. For the righteous, the path is lit like the dawn. For the wicked, the path is filled with darkness, and they stumble through it. Let us walk in the light, with the pungent aroma of righteousness.

---

[94] Proverbs 4:18-19 (AMP).

Chapter Five – The Fool

(Days 50-63, Dhammapada 60-75)

Chapter Five focuses on the foolish man's life. We ought not to keep company with fools as they may influence us to do evil. The foolish are complacent and prone to self-conceit. The fool thinks doing an evil deed is sweet, but afterwards suffers for it.

Sooner or later our foolish actions catch up to us, so we ought to seek after wisdom and knowledge and put aside foolish, reckless behavior.

Day 50

Solomon (950 BCE)

I have seen everything during my lifetime of futility; there is a righteous man who perishes in his righteousness and there is a wicked man who prolongs his life in his wickedness.[95]

Buddha (525 BCE)

[60] Long is the night to him who is awake; long is a mile to him who is tired; long is life to the foolish who do not know the true law.

A foolish man's life, if it is miraculously extended in spite of his foolishness, seems even longer to him, punctuated with obstacles and difficulties brought upon himself. We can avoid that kind of long, painful life, by keeping the law ever before us.

---

[95] Ecclesiastes 7:15 (NASB).

Day 51

Solomon

Buddha

He who walks with wise men will be wise, but the companion of fools will be destroyed.[96]

Go from the presence of a foolish man, when you do not perceive in him the lips of knowledge.[97]

[61] If a traveller [sic] does not meet with one who is his better, or his equal, let him firmly keep to his solitary journey; there is no companionship with a fool.

It is better for us to be in the company of the wise or even to be alone, than to keep company with fools. If we make a fool our companion, we will not find him speaking with knowledge or wisdom, and we may be put in jeopardy by his foolish ways. If we seek out the company of the wise, we will grow in wisdom.

[96] Proverbs 13:20 (NKJV).
[97] Proverbs 14:7 (NKJV).

Day 52

Solomon

Man is a mere phantom as he goes to and fro: He bustles about, but only in vain; he heaps up wealth, not knowing who will get it.[98]

To the man who pleases him, God gives wisdom, knowledge and happiness, but to the sinner he gives the task of gathering and storing up wealth to hand it over to the one who pleases God. This too is meaningless, a chasing after the wind.[99]

Buddha

[62] "These sons belong to me, and this wealth belongs to me," with such thoughts a fool is tormented. He himself does not belong to himself; how much less sons and wealth?

As we hurry through our lives, thinking our families and wealth belong to us, we forget that we all die and can take nothing with us. Whatever we build up in this life, goes to another after we die. Let us gather wisdom and knowledge, which is a better path.

[98] Psalm 39:6 (NIV), a psalm of King David, Solomon's father.
[99] Ecclesiastes 2:26 (NIV).

Day 53

Solomon

Do you see a man wise in his own eyes? There is more hope for a fool than for him.[100]

He who trusts in himself is a fool, but he who walks in wisdom is kept safe.[101]

Buddha

[63] The fool who knows his foolishness, is wise at least so far. But a fool who thinks himself wise, he is called a fool indeed.

Self-conceit is unpleasant in anyone, and it is not productive in our lives. We ought to think of ourselves as seekers of wisdom, not as someone who has arrived at the end of the journey and is all puffed up with their conquest. Let us walk in wisdom and the safety it provides.

---

[100] Proverbs 26:12 (NASB).
[101] Proverbs 28:26 (NIV).

Day 54

Solomon

It is as sport to a [self-confident] fool to do wickedness, but to have skillful and godly Wisdom is pleasure and relaxation to a man of understanding.[102]

A fool finds pleasure in evil conduct, but a man of understanding delights in wisdom.[103]

Buddha

[64] If a fool be associated with a wise man even all his life, he will perceive the truth as little as a spoon perceives the taste of soup.

The choices we make in friendship and in our actions define us as people. Will we choose a wise or a foolish friend? Our friends influence us, often when we are not aware of it. Will we relish doing evil as though it was a competitive sport? Will we seek out wisdom and do good in our lives? Every day, these are ongoing choices for us to make.

---

[102] Proverbs 10:23 (AMP).
[103] Proverbs 10:23 (NIV).

Day 55

Solomon

Buddha

He who walks with the wise grows wise, but a companion of fools suffers harm.[104]

Give instruction to a wise man, and he will be still wiser; teach a just man, and he will increase in learning.[105]

[65] If an intelligent man be associated for one minute only with a wise man, he will soon perceive the truth, as the tongue perceives the taste of soup.

One moment with a wise man is more profitable than a lifetime with a fool. Let us seek out the company of the wise, so that we will grow in wisdom.

---

[104] Proverbs 13:20 (NIV).
[105] Proverbs 9:9 (NKJV).

Day 56

Solomon

Buddha

Since they hated knowledge and did not choose to fear the LORD, since they would not accept my advice and spurned my rebuke, they will eat the fruit of their ways and be filled with the fruit of their schemes. For the waywardness of the simple will kill them, and the complacency of fools will destroy them.[106]

[66] Fools of little understanding have themselves for their greatest enemies, for they do evil deeds which must bear bitter fruits.

Being complacent (extremely self-satisfied, already defined earlier as being foolish) and wayward (wanting to have our own way, regardless of the wishes or good of others) lead to heartache and destruction. When we behave that way, we are our own worst enemy. Seeking wisdom and knowledge is an active task involving humility and diligence. It takes effort. Let us choose the wiser path and walk it in perseverance.

---

[106] Proverbs 1:29-31 (NIV).

Day 57

Solomon	**Buddha**

If you are wise, your wisdom will reward you; if you are a mocker, you alone will suffer.[107]

[67] That deed is not well done of which a man must repent, and the reward of which he receives crying and with a tearful face.

Evil pursues sinners, but to the righteous, good shall be repaid.[108]

[68] No, that deed is well done of which a man does not repent, and the reward of which he receives gladly and cheerfully.

Our actions create results, and those results reward us for good or bad. When we do evil, we reap the result of it in tears. When we do good, we reap the reward in gladness. The Apostle Paul wrote to the Galatians, ". . . a man reaps what he sows."[109]

---

[107] Proverbs 9:12 (NIV).
[108] Proverbs 13:21 (NKJV).
[109] Galatians 6:7b (NIV).

Day 58

Solomon	Buddha
Food gained by deceit is sweet to a man, but afterward his mouth will be filled with gravel.[110]	[69] As long as the evil deed done does not bear fruit, the fool thinks it is like honey; but when it ripens, then the fool suffers grief.

Initially we might think that doing an evil deed is sweet, but afterwards, we suffer from it, like eating a mouthful of gravel instead of honey. Afterwards, the consequences of our actions come to fruition or become public, and then they become distasteful.

Day 59

Solomon	Buddha
Wise men store up knowledge, but the mouth of a fool invites ruin.[111] The fear of the LORD is the beginning of knowledge, but fools despise wisdom and instruction.[112]	[70] Let a fool month after month eat his food (like an ascetic) with the tip of a blade of Kusa grass, yet he is not worth the sixteenth particle of those who have well weighed the law.

When we only consider ourselves and what will satisfy our needs and desires, we are foolish and lack the humility to accept instruction. When we store up knowledge and wisdom, and meditate on the law, we are wise.

---

[110] Proverbs 20:17 (AMP).
[111] Proverbs 10:14 (NIV).
[112] Proverbs 1:7 (NKJV).

Day 60

Solomon

Buddha

What the wicked fears will come upon him, but the desire of the righteous will be granted.[113]

[71] An evil deed, like newly-drawn milk, does not turn (suddenly); smouldering [*sic*], like fire covered by ashes, it follows the fool.

The evil deeds of a wicked man ensnare him; the cords of his sin hold him fast.[114]

[72] And when the evil deed, after it has become known, brings sorrow to the fool, then it destroys his bright lot, nay, it cleaves his head.

It doesn't always happen immediately, but everything we do has repercussions. Sooner or later, the repercussions of our deeds catch up with us. If we have behaved with integrity and done good deeds, the results are for the better, but if we have done evil, it can turn upon us like being caught in a suddenly turning fire.

---

[113] Proverbs 10:24 (NASB).
[114] Proverbs 5:22 (NIV).

Day 61

Solomon	Buddha

Do not exalt yourself in the presence of the king, and do not stand in the place of the great; for it is better that he say to you, "Come up here," than that you should be put lower in the presence of the prince, whom your eyes have seen.[115]

[73] Let the fool wish for a false reputation, for precedence among the Bhikshus, for lordship in the convents, for worship among other people!

A false reputation is a snare. If we exaggerate our accomplishments or attributes, we will be found out. Better to be humble in our estimation of ourselves, and have someone else lift us up, than to think more highly than we should and be put in our place.

---

[115] Proverbs 25:6-7 (NKJV).

Day 62

Solomon	Buddha

Solomon

Pride goes before destruction, a haughty spirit before a fall.[116]

A man's pride brings him low, but a man of lowly spirit gains honor.[117]

The proud and arrogant man—"Mocker" is his name; he behaves with overweening pride.[118]

Buddha

[74] "May both the layman and he who has left the world think that this is done by me; may they be subject to me in everything which is to be done or is not to be done," thus is the mind of the fool, and his desire and pride increase.

Having excessive pride in our abilities and achievements, and wanting others to think we have accomplished more than we actually have is vanity. Better to be of a humble spirit thinking rightly about our actions, than to be put in our place for being arrogant.

---

[116] Proverbs 16:18 (NIV).
[117] Proverbs 29:23 (NIV).
[118] Proverbs 21:24 (NIV).

Day 63

Solomon	**Buddha**

Wealth is worthless in the day of wrath, but righteousness delivers from death.[119]

For God gives wisdom and knowledge and joy to a man who is good in His sight; but to the sinner He gives the work of gathering and collecting, that he may give to him who is good before God. This also is vanity and grasping for the wind.[120]

[75] "One is the road that leads to wealth, another the road that leads to Nirvana;" if the Bhikshu, the disciple of Buddha, has learnt this, he will not yearn for honour [sic], he will strive after separation from the world.

Each of us has the choice before us of striving for wealth and honor in this life or of investing our energy in gathering knowledge and wisdom, and walking a righteous path. On this topic, Jesus said,

> No one can serve two masters. Either he will hate the one and love the other, or he will be devoted to the one and despise the other. You cannot serve both God and Money.[121]

---

[119] Proverbs 11:4 (NIV).
[120] Ecclesiastes 2:26 (NKJV).
[121] Matthew 6:24 (NIV).

Chapter Six – The Wise Man (Pandita)

(Days 64-76, Dhammapada 76-89)

The last chapter discussed the fool. In contrast, this chapter describes the wise man. A wise man gives good advice and reproves rightly. His counsel is like sweet perfume. He is a friend to be desired. He drinks in the law and lives happily with a serene mind. He is as solid as a rock and is not shaken by the winds of praise or blame.

He avoids extremes and goes through life on an even keel. He conquers his appetites. He avoids envying others and chasing after the material things of this world. His mind is well-grounded in knowledge, and death holds no power over him, because his hope is in something greater.

Day 64

Solomon (950 BCE)

Ointment and perfume delight the heart, and the sweetness of a man's friend does so by hearty counsel.[122]

Iron sharpens iron, so one man sharpens another.[123]

Faithful are the wounds of a friend, but the kisses of an enemy are deceitful.[124]

Buddha (525 BCE)

[76] If you see an intelligent man who tells you where true treasures are to be found, who shows what is to be avoided, and administers reproofs, follow that wise man; it will be better, not worse, for those who follow him.

An intelligent, wise man who gives good advice, who cautions us about things to avoid, and who reproves us rightly, is a friend to be desired. Even if he wounds us, it is from faithfulness in friendship. A friend who gives good counsel is like sweet perfume in our lives.

---

[122] Proverbs 27:9 (NKJV).
[123] Proverbs 27:17 (NASB).
[124] Proverbs 27:6 (NKJV).

Day 65

Solomon

Do not rebuke a mocker or he will hate you; rebuke a wise man and he will love you.[125]

Pride only breeds quarrels, but wisdom is found in those who take advice.[126]

He who scorns instruction will pay for it, but he who respects a command is rewarded.[127]

Buddha

[77] Let him admonish, let him teach, let him forbid what is improper!—he will be beloved of the good, by the bad he will be hated.

If we respond to the instruction given by a wise teacher, we will in turn love the teacher for his guidance. However, if we scorn instruction, we will hate the teacher, and behaving in our ignorant state, we will suffer for our actions.

---

[125] Proverbs 9:8 (NIV).
[126] Proverbs 13:10 (NIV).
[127] Proverbs 13:13 (NIV).

Day 66

Solomon	**Buddha**
The righteous should choose his friends carefully, for the way of the wicked leads them astray.[128]	[78] Do not have evil-doers for friends, do not have low people for friends: have virtuous people for friends, have for friends the best of men.

We must be careful in choosing friends, because companionship with those who do evil leads us down the wrong path. Righteous, wise friends will enhance our lives, not jeopardize them.

Day 67

Solomon	**Buddha**
Those who love Your law have great peace, and nothing causes them to stumble.[129] Direct me in the path of your commands, for there I find delight.[130]	[79] He who drinks in the law lives happily with a serene mind: the sage rejoices always in the law, as preached by the elect (Ariyas).

Meditating on the law, delighting in and loving the law, drinking it in deeply, if we do these things we will live with great peace of mind, and we will not stumble.

---

[128] Proverbs 12:26 (NKJV).
[129] Psalm 119:165 (NASB).
[130] Psalm 119:35 (NIV).

Day 68

Solomon

Buddha

Instruct a wise man and he will be wiser still; teach a righteous man and he will add to his learning.[131]

Wise men store up knowledge, but with the mouth of the foolish, ruin is at hand.[132]

A wise man's heart guides his mouth, and his lips promote instruction.[133]

[80] Well-makers lead the water (wherever they like); fletchers bend the arrow; carpenters bend a log of wood; wise people fashion themselves.

A wise man is proactive in his learning and in how he conducts his life. If we are eager to learn, store up knowledge, and mindfully direct our speech and actions, we will be like an expert craftsman bending lumber to make a fine piece of furniture.

---

[131] Proverbs 9:9 (NIV).
[132] Proverbs 10:14 (NASB).
[133] Proverbs 16:23 (NIV).

Day 69

Solomon

Buddha

The wicked are overthrown
and are no more, but the
house of the righteous will
stand.[134]

[81] As a solid rock is not
shaken by the wind, wise
people falter not amidst
blame and praise.

    The wise have a foundation in knowledge and the law, and are not shaken by opinion, even if it flatters. Foolish people flounder when faced with diverse opinions. When we are faced with the winds of opinion, whether they be positive or negative, praise or blame, we need not falter or be shaken.

---

[134] Proverbs 12:7 (NKJV).

Day 70

Solomon

Buddha

Those who love Your law
have great peace, and
nothing causes them to
stumble.[135]

[82] Wise people, after they
have listened to the laws,
become serene, like a deep,
smooth, and still lake.

How sweet are Your words to
my taste, sweeter than
honey to my mouth![136]

The fear of the LORD leads to
life: Then one rests content,
untouched by trouble.[137]

We all desire to be at peace, untouched by trouble. As we read and meditate on the law, it is sweet like honey to our taste, and we can rest content in the wisdom and security of it.

---

[135] Psalm 119:165 (NASB).
[136] Psalm 119:103 (NKJV).
[137] Proverbs 19:23 (NIV).

Day 71

Solomon	Buddha

Do not be overrighteous, neither be overwise—why destroy yourself? Do not be overwicked, and do not be a fool—why die before your time? It is good to grasp the one and not let go of the other. The man who fears God will avoid all extremes.[138]

[83] Good people walk on whatever befall, the good do not prattle, longing for pleasure; whether touched by happiness or sorrow wise people never appear elated or depressed.

The expression, to walk on an even keel, comes from seamen attempting to walk on a ship that is pitching in the water. It means to walk steadily, as though walking on the keel, which is the principal beam or structure running lengthwise along the center of the ship from bow to stern, to which the frame is attached. We can avoid extremes and walk on an even keel whether joy or sorrow comes our way.

---

[138] Ecclesiastes 7:16-18 (NIV).

Day 72

Solomon

Buddha

Two things I ask of you, O LORD; do not refuse me before I die: Keep falsehood and lies far from me; give me neither poverty nor riches, but give me only my daily bread. Otherwise, I may have too much and disown you and say, "Who is the LORD?" Or I may become poor and steal, and so dishonor the name of my God.[139]

These [sinful] men lie in wait for their own blood; they ambush only themselves! Such are the paths of all who go after ill-gotten gain; it takes away the life of those who get it.[140]

[84] If, whether for his own sake, or for the sake of others, a man wishes neither for a son, nor for wealth, nor for lordship, and if he does not wish for his own success by unfair means, then he is good, wise, and virtuous.

We ought not to desire success derived by unfair means. Any success that comes our way ought to be accomplished by being good, wise and virtuous. If we are in a position of authority, let us carry out our duties with wisdom and righteousness. Let us not be driven by desire for an unfair advantage, or for wealth or prestige.

---

[139] Proverbs 30:7-9 (NIV). Proverbs 30 is attributed to Agur, son of Jakeh.
[140] Proverbs 1:18-19 (NIV).

Day 73

Solomon	Buddha
Most men will proclaim each his own goodness, but who can find a faithful man?[141] The truly righteous man attains life, but he who pursues evil goes to his death.[142]	[85] Few are there among men who arrive at the other shore (become Arhats) [have attained Nirvana]; the other people here run up and down the shore.

Faithful men are rare and hard to find. Such men are truly righteous. Righteous men attain life and evildoers die. A storm of trouble will kill the wicked, while the righteous stand firm. Rather than running up and down following the winds of opinion, we do well to follow the law, for those who follow the law are spared.

Day 74

Solomon	Buddha
When the storm has swept by, the wicked are gone, but the righteous stand firm forever.[143]	[86] But those who, when the law has been well preached to them, follow the law, will pass across the dominion of death, however difficult to overcome.

Death holds no power over the righteous, because their hope is in something greater. The storms of life will pass by them as they stand firm.

---

[141] Proverbs 20:6 (NKJV).
[142] Proverbs 11:19 (NIV).
[143] Proverbs 10:25 (NIV).

Day 75

Solomon	Buddha

The desire of the righteous ends only in good, but the hope of the wicked ends only in wrath.[144]

Do they not err who devise evil and wander from the way of life? But loving-kindness and mercy, loyalty and faithfulness, shall be to those who devise good.[145]

[87, 88.] A wise man should leave the dark state (of ordinary life), and follow the bright state (of the Bhikshu). After going from his home to a homeless state, he should in his retirement look for enjoyment where there seemed to be no enjoyment. Leaving all pleasures behind, and calling nothing his own, the wise man should purge himself from all the troubles of the mind.

We ought to leave the ordinary path of being burdened by possessions, and live in a state of freedom from belongings. They should not rule our life. Walking a pure and righteous path will bring about good, and result in a life filled with kindness, mercy, loyalty and faithfulness.

---

[144] Proverbs 11:23 (NIV).
[145] Proverbs 14:22 (AMP).

Day 76

Solomon

. . . cast off the troubles of your body, for youth and vigor are meaningless.[146]

Better one handful with tranquility than two handfuls with toil and chasing after the wind.[147]

A sound heart is life to the body, but envy is rottenness to the bones.[148]

Buddha

[89] Those whose mind is well grounded in the (seven) elements of knowledge, who without clinging to anything, rejoice in freedom from attachment, whose appetites have been conquered, and who are full of light, are free (even) in this world.

Conquering our appetites, we do well to ground our minds in knowledge, avoiding envy of others and chasing after the material things of this world. Then, our minds will be tranquil and full of light, and we will experience freedom.

---

[146] Ecclesiastes 11:10b (NIV).
[147] Ecclesiastes 4:6 (NIV).
[148] Proverbs 14:30 (NKJV).

Chapter Seven – The Venerable (Arhat)
(Days 77-86, Dhammapada 90-99)

This chapter continues with those worthy of respect, the venerable. They pursue a meditative, simple life. They abstain from seeking wealth and self-gratification. Their thought life is restrained, and they are content.

The venerable subdue appetites and desires, and are free from pride. Where they dwell is delightful, and they bless all around them.

Day 77

Solomon (950 BCE)

When calamity comes, the wicked are brought down, but even in death the righteous have a refuge.[149]

Buddha (525 BCE)

[90] There is no suffering for him who has finished his journey, and abandoned grief, who has freed himself on all sides, and thrown off all fetters.

As we finish out this life, if we have done well to gather knowledge and wisdom and to walk a pure and righteous path, we will be free from the suffering and calamity that the wicked endure, having done evil all their lives.

Day 78

Solomon

A good name is better than precious ointment [or perfume], and the day of death than the day of one's birth.[150]

Buddha

[91] They depart with their thoughts well-collected, they are not happy in their abode; like swans who have left their lake, they leave their house and home.

Leaving this body at the point of death is like leaving a house we no longer want to live in, and if we have lived a righteous life, the day of our death will be even better than the day we were born.

---

[149] Proverbs 14:32 (NIV).
[150] Ecclesiastes 7:1 (NKJV).

Day 79

Solomon	**Buddha**

Better is the poor who walks in his integrity than one who is perverse in his lips, and is a fool.[151]

Better is a little with righteousness than great income with injustice.[152]

[92] Men who have no riches, who live on recognised [sic] food, who have perceived void and unconditioned freedom (Nirvana), their path is difficult to understand, like that of birds in the air.

An ascetic life, where we pursue a meditative, simple life, and we abstain from seeking wealth and self-gratification, may be hard to understand for our friends and family.

---

[151] Proverbs 19:1 (NKJV).
[152] Proverbs 16:8 (NASB).

Day 80

Solomon	**Buddha**
Better is the little that the [uncompromisingly] righteous have than the abundance [of possessions] of many who are wrong and wicked.[153]	[93] He whose appetites are stilled, who is not absorbed in enjoyment, who has perceived void and unconditioned freedom (Nirvana), his path is difficult to understand, like that of birds in the air.
The righteousness of the upright delivers them, but the unfaithful are trapped by evil desires.[154]	

When our appetites are restrained, even a little may seem like a great abundance. How much better to have little than to be trapped by evil desires.

---

[153] Psalm 37:16 (AMP), a psalm of King David, Solomon's father.
[154] Proverbs 11:6 (NIV).

Day 81

Solomon	Buddha
Better to be lowly in spirit along with the oppressed than to share plunder with the proud.[155] Better what the eye sees than the roving of the appetite. This too is meaningless, a chasing after the wind.[156]	[94] The gods even envy him whose senses, like horses well broken in by the driver, have been subdued, who is free from pride, and free from appetites.

Our appetites and desires can overrun us and rule our lives like a horse that has not been broken in and who bolts away with its rider. Let us subdue them and be free from pride and the ruling nature of our appetites and desires.

Day 82

Solomon	Buddha
He who leans on, trusts in, and is confident in his riches shall fall, but the [uncompromisingly] righteous shall flourish like a green bough.[157]	[95] Such a one who does his duty is tolerant like the earth, like Indra's bolt; he is like a lake without mud; no new births are in store for him.

We can trust in accumulating wealth, or we can focus on living a righteous life. Better to live righteously and have peace like a clear, calm lake.

---

[155] Proverbs 16:19 (NIV).
[156] Ecclesiastes 6:9 (NIV).
[157] Proverbs 11:28 (AMP).

Day 83

Solomon

Buddha

The quiet words of the wise are more to be heeded than the shouts of a ruler of fools.[158]

So then, banish anxiety from your heart and cast off the troubles of your body.[159]

My heart is not proud, O LORD, my eyes are not haughty; I do not concern myself with great matters or things too wonderful for me. But I have stilled and quieted my soul; like a weaned child with its mother, like a weaned child is my soul within me.[160]

[96] His thought is quiet, quiet are his word and deed, when he has obtained freedom by true knowledge, when he has thus become a quiet man.

Being quiet is a very difficult thing in our modern society. Consider quiet as a necessity like air and water. Our minds and bodies require some quiet to restrain our thoughts and banish our anxieties. Let us seek after a still, quiet soul and mind, like a child who has been nourished and is content to rest in its mother's arms.

---

[158] Ecclesiastes 9:17 (NIV).
[159] Ecclesiastes 11:10a (NIV).
[160] Psalm 131:1-2 (NIV), a psalm of King David, Solomon's father.

Day 84

Solomon

Buddha

My son, if sinners entice you, do not consent. If they say, "Come with us, let us lie in wait to shed blood; let us lurk secretly for the innocent without cause; let us swallow them alive like Sheol, and whole, like those who go down to the Pit; we shall find all kinds of precious possessions, we shall fill our houses with spoil; cast in your lot among us, let us all have one purse"—My son, do not walk in the way with them, keep your foot from their path; for their feet run to evil, and they make haste to shed blood.[161]

[97] The man who is free from credulity, but knows the uncreated, who has cut all ties, removed all temptations, renounced all desires, he is the greatest of men.

If we are quick to believe others and are gullible and overly trusting, we may fall into a trap of being tempted by others and find ourselves indulging in temptations and being drawn in by evil desires. Let us be free from credulity and putting our trust in others, where it is not deserved.

---

[161] Proverbs 1:10-16 (NKJV).

Day 85

Solomon	Buddha
When the righteous prosper, the city rejoices; when the wicked perish, there are shouts of joy.[162]	[98] In a hamlet or in a forest, in the deep water or on the dry land, wherever venerable persons (Arhanta) dwell, that place is delightful.

It is not where we live, but how we live that makes a difference. Wherever a righteous, venerable person lives is a delightful place. He flourishes and all around him benefit and rejoice. With wisdom and knowledge, let us walk carefully through our journey, and it will be a blessing to all around us.

---

[162] Proverbs 11:10 (NIV).

Day 86

Solomon

The heart of the wise is in the house of mourning, but the heart of fools is in the house of pleasure.[163]

He who loves pleasure will become a poor man; he who loves wine and oil will not become rich.[164]

Buddha

[99] Forests are delightful; where the world finds no delight, there the passionless will find delight, for they look not for pleasures.

If we let it, being hedonistic will consume our lives like an addiction. The pursuit of pleasure turns us into fools, whether it be sensual desires, the hunger for fine foods, or lusting after monetary gain or prestige. Let us be wise and seek after a greater delight, a meditative, righteous life.

---

[163] Ecclesiastes 7:4 (NIV).
[164] Proverbs 21:17 (NASB).

R. E. Sherman

Chapter Eight – The Thousands

(Days 87-96, Dhammapada 100-115)

Chapter Eight portrays contrasts in life often using large numbers. For example, one word of sense is better than a thousand senseless words. A man who conquers himself is better than one who conquers thousands.

Sacrifice to gain merit or prestige is not worth a fraction of doing the right thing, and one day of a righteous life is better than a hundred years of one who is idle and weak.

These comparisons all point to the better choice: choosing to live a righteous life.

Day 87

Solomon (950 BCE)

Death and life are in the power of the tongue, and they who indulge in it shall eat the fruit of it [for death or life].[165]

The quiet words of the wise are more to be heeded than the shouts of a ruler of fools.[166]

He who has knowledge spares his words, and a man of understanding is of a calm spirit. Even a fool is counted wise when he holds his peace; when he shuts his lips, he is considered perceptive.[167]

Buddha (525 BCE)

[100] Even though a speech be a thousand (of words), but made up of senseless words, one word of sense is better, which if a man hears, he becomes quiet.

The tongue is powerful, for good or for evil. We are better off to speak a few words of sense, than to prattle on aimlessly and be found a fool.

---

[165] Proverbs 18:21 (AMP).
[166] Ecclesiastes 9:17 (NIV).
[167] Proverbs 17:27-28 (NKJV).

Day 88

Solomon

Buddha

The more the words, the less the meaning, and how does that profit anyone?[168]

The words of a wise man's mouth are gracious, but the lips of a fool shall swallow him up.[169]

Reckless words pierce like a sword, but the tongue of the wise brings healing.[170]

[101] Even though a Gatha (poem) be a thousand (of words), but made up of senseless words, one word of a Gatha is better, which if a man hears, he becomes quiet.

[102] Though a man recite a hundred Gathas made up of senseless words, one word of the law is better, which if a man hears, he becomes quiet.

More is not always better. A single word of the law accomplishes more in our lives than thousands of words of meaningless chatter. Let us be measured in our speech to one another. Let our words be gracious, full of wisdom and good will.

---

[168] Ecclesiastes 6:11 (NIV).
[169] Ecclesiastes 10:12 (NKJV).
[170] Proverbs 12:18 (NIV).

Day 89

Solomon	Buddha
He who is slow to anger is better than the mighty. And he who rules his spirit than he who takes a city.[171]	[103] If one man conquer in battle a thousand times thousand men, and if another conquer himself, he is the greatest of conquerors.

The value of conquering ourselves is greater than that of winning a war. Let us discipline our thoughts and emotions like a soldier following orders on the battlefield.

Day 90

Solomon	Buddha
Listen to advice and accept discipline, and at the end you will be counted among the wise.[172]	[104, 105.] One's own self conquered is better than all other people; not even a god, a Gandharva, not Mara with Brahman could change into defeat the victory of a man who has vanquished himself, and always lives under restraint.
He who is slow to anger is better than the mighty, he who rules his [own] spirit than he who takes a city.[173]	

Without self-control, we are like a broken down city with no walls of protection or fortification. It takes little to defeat us. But if we truly subdue ourselves, we are more victorious than a conquering army.

---

[171] Proverbs 16:32 (NKJV).
[172] Proverbs 19:20 (NIV).
[173] Proverbs 16:32 (AMP).

Day 91

Solomon	Buddha

To do what is right and just is more acceptable to the LORD than sacrifice.[174]

[106] If a man for a hundred years sacrifice month after month with a thousand, and if he but for one moment pay homage to a man whose soul is grounded (in true knowledge), better is that homage than sacrifice for a hundred years.

Keep your foot [give your mind to what you are doing] when you go [as Jacob to sacred Bethel] to the house of God. For to draw near to hear and obey is better than to give the sacrifice of fools [carelessly, irreverently] too ignorant to know that they are doing evil.[175]

[107] If a man for a hundred years worship Agni (fire) in the forest, and if he but for one moment pay homage to a man whose soul is grounded (in true knowledge), better is that homage than sacrifice for a hundred years.

We can get caught up in traditions and making sacrifices in our lives, especially sacrifices of a material nature. Let us guard ourselves from meaningless, repetitious sacrifice, and actively do that which is good.

---

[174] Proverbs 21:3 (NIV).
[175] Ecclesiastes 5:1 (AMP).

Day 92

Solomon	Buddha
To do righteousness and justice is desired by the LORD more than sacrifice.[176]	[108] Whatever a man sacrifice in this world as an offering or as an oblation for a whole year in order to gain merit, the whole of it is not worth a quarter (a farthing); reverence shown to the righteous is better.

Sacrifice to gain merit or prestige is not worth a fraction of doing the right thing, acting in a just manner, or being reverent to the righteous. Let any sacrifices be done with a pure heart, and let righteousness and justice be more the desirable path.

Day 93

Solomon	Buddha
He who oppresses the poor shows contempt for their Maker, but whoever is kind to the needy honors God.[177] He who pursues righteousness and love finds life, prosperity and honor.[178]	[109] He who always greets and constantly reveres the aged, four things will increase to him, viz. life, beauty, happiness, power.

If we have reverence for our elders and are kind to the needy, we find our lives overflowing with life, beauty, and happiness.

---

[176] Proverbs 21:3 (NASB).
[177] Proverbs 14:31 (NIV).
[178] Proverbs 21:21 (NIV).

Day 94

Solomon	Buddha
Better a poor and wise youth than an old and foolish king who will be admonished no more.[179]	[110] But he who lives a hundred years, vicious and unrestrained, a life of one day is better if a man is virtuous and reflecting.
Better is one day in your courts than a thousand elsewhere; I would rather be a doorkeeper in the house of my God than dwell in the tents of the wicked.[180]	[111] And he who lives a hundred years, ignorant and unrestrained, a life of one day is better if a man is wise and reflecting.

A single day of a virtuous reflective life is far better than to live a long, unrestrained life, full of wickedness. Let us be mindful of the way we spend our energy and our days.

---

[179] Ecclesiastes 4:13 (NKJV).
[180] Psalm 84:10 (NIV).

Day 95

Solomon

So I said, "Wisdom is better than strength."[181]

His pleasure is not in the strength of the horse, nor his delight in the legs of a man; the LORD delights in those who fear him, who put their hope in his unfailing love.[182]

Blessed is the man who listens to me [wisdom], watching daily at my gates, waiting at the posts of my doors. For whoever finds me finds life, and obtains favor from the LORD; but he who sins against me wrongs his own soul; all those who hate me love death.[183]

Buddha

[112] And he who lives a hundred years, idle and weak, a life of one day is better if a man has attained firm strength.

[113] And he who lives a hundred years, not seeing beginning and end, a life of one day is better if a man sees beginning and end.

We do better to contemplate life from birth to death and actively seek wisdom, than to put our trust in being physically strong and are foolish in the process.

---

[181] Ecclesiastes 9:16a (NASB).
[182] Psalm 147:10-11 (NIV).
[183] Proverbs 8:34-36 (NKJV).

Day 96

Solomon

Buddha

Better is one day in your courts than a thousand elsewhere; I would rather be a doorkeeper in the house of my God than dwell in the tents of the wicked.[184]

When I consider Your heavens, the work of Your fingers, the moon and the stars, which You have ordained, What is man that You are mindful of him, and the son of man that You visit him?[185]

The fear of the LORD prolongs life, but the years of the wicked will be shortened.[186]

[114] And he who lives a hundred years, not seeing the immortal place, a life of one day is better if a man sees the immortal place.

[115] And he who lives a hundred years, not seeing the highest law, a life of one day is better if a man sees the highest law.

Seeing the spiritual, seeing and knowing the law, seeing that life is more than the physical existence we have on this planet, is very important. Better it is to "see" for one day than to live for hundreds of years in blindness to spiritual life.

---

[184] Psalm 84:10 (NIV).
[185] Psalm 8:3-4 (NKJV), a psalm of King David, Solomon's father.
[186] Proverbs 10:27 (NASB).

R. E. Sherman

Chapter Nine – Evil

(Days 97-106, Dhammapada 116-128)

This chapter outlines the need to avoid evil and not to let it become a habit. It is better to make doing good a habit.

The evil-doer will think he is happy until his evil acts have come to fruition. Far better to delight in leading a righteous life. Like avoiding a dangerous road or not touching poison, we ought to avoid evil.

There isn't anywhere on earth that we can avoid death, because death awaits us all. Contemplating this, we ought to earnestly seek to live a righteous life and avoid doing evil.

Day 97

Solomon (950 BCE)

Do not withhold good from those who deserve it, when it is in your power to act. Do not say to your neighbor, "Come back later; I'll give it tomorrow"—when you now have it with you.[187]

Buddha (525 BCE)

[116] If a man would hasten towards the good, he should keep his thought away from evil; if a man does what is good slothfully, his mind delights in evil.

Holding back from doing good, opens the door to doing evil. We ought to hasten to do good, whenever it is in our power to do so.

Day 98

Solomon

It is as sport to a [self-confident] fool to do wickedness, but to have skillful and godly Wisdom is pleasure and relaxation to a man of understanding.[188]

Buddha

[117] If a man commits a sin, let him not do it again; let him not delight in sin: pain is the outcome of evil.

If we commit a sin, we should not let it become a habit, doing it over and over again. A man of understanding delights and takes pleasure in wisdom and the law, not in doing evil.

---

[187] Proverbs 3:27–28 (NIV).
[188] Proverb 10:23 (AMP).

Day 99

Solomon	Buddha
I know that there is nothing better for men than to be happy and do good while they live.[189]	[118] If a man does what is good, let him do it again; let him delight in it: happiness is the outcome of good.
Will they not go astray who devise evil? But kindness and truth will be to those who devise good.[190]	

Do good, and do it again and again. Make it a habit. Buddha said, the outcome would be happiness. Solomon knew of no better way for a man to live, and King David said to, "Turn from evil and do good; seek peace and pursue it."[191]

---

[189] Ecclesiastes 3:12 (NIV).
[190] Proverbs 14:22 (NASB).
[191] Psalm 34:14 (NIV), a psalm of King David, Solomon's father.

Day 100

Solomon

A fool finds pleasure in evil conduct, but a man of understanding delights in wisdom. What the wicked dreads will overtake him; what the righteous desire will be granted. When the storm has swept by, the wicked are gone, but the righteous stand firm forever.[192]

He who earnestly seeks after and craves righteousness, mercy, and loving-kindness will find life in addition to righteousness (uprightness and right standing with God) and honor.[193]

Buddha

[119] Even an evil-doer sees happiness as long as his evil deed has not ripened; but when his evil deed has ripened, then does the evil-doer see evil.

[120] Even a good man sees evil days, as long as his good deed has not ripened; but when his good deed has ripened, then does the good man see happy days.

It is foolish to take pleasure in doing evil. When we do evil, what we dread will come to fruition. We will be washed away as though in a storm. The better path is to delight in leading a righteous life. In that, we can weather life's difficulties. In doing good, we will reap wisdom, knowledge, and happiness.

---

[192] Proverb 10:23-25 (NIV).
[193] Proverb 21:21 (AMP).

Day 101

Solomon

Buddha

Like a muddied fountain and a polluted spring is a righteous man who yields, falls down, and compromises his integrity before the wicked.[194]

He who earnestly seeks good finds favor, but trouble will come to him who seeks evil.[195]

The prudent see danger and take refuge, but the simple keep going and pay the penalty.[196]

[121] Let no man think lightly of evil, saying in his heart, It will not come nigh unto me. Even by the falling of water-drops a water-pot is filled; the fool becomes full of evil, even if he gather it little by little.

[122] Let no man think lightly of good, saying in his heart, It will not come nigh unto me. Even by the falling of water-drops a water-pot is filled; the wise man becomes full of good, even if he gather it little by little.

If we allow evil to slowly gather in our lives, we are like a spring becoming muddied and polluted. Let us keep ourselves unpolluted by even the smallest acts of evil. Instead, let us fill our lives each day by earnestly seeking to do good. Then, we will be like the water-pot filled drop by drop every day until we are overflowing with righteousness and integrity.

---

[194] Proverbs 25:26 (AMP).
[195] Proverbs 11:27 (NKJV).
[196] Proverbs 27:12 (NIV).

Day 102

Solomon

Buddha

The highway of the upright avoids evil; he who guards his way guards his life.[197]

[123] Let a man avoid evil deeds, as a merchant, if he has few companions and carries much wealth, avoids a dangerous road; as a man who loves life avoids poison.

A merchant traveling alone with a great deal of money will be very careful to avoid a dangerous road, as a man who loves life will avoid drinking poison. We ought to avoid evil and guard our way, as though guarding our very existence.

---

[197] Proverbs 16:17 (NIV).

Day 103

Solomon

Buddha

My son, preserve sound judgment and discernment, do not let them out of your sight; they will be life for you, an ornament to grace your neck. Then you will go on your way in safety, and your foot will not stumble; when you lie down, you will not be afraid; when you lie down, your sleep will be sweet.[198]

He hides away sound and godly Wisdom and stores it for the righteous (those who are upright and in right standing with Him); He is a shield to those who walk uprightly and in integrity.[199]

[124] He who has no wound on his hand, may touch poison with his hand; poison does not affect one who has no wound; nor is there evil for one who does not commit evil.

If we have integrity and sound judgment, and are undefiled by evil, coming into contact with evil cannot wound us, just as poison cannot affect the unwounded hand. The Apostle Paul wrote, "Unto the pure all things are pure: but unto them that are defiled and unbelieving is nothing pure; but even their mind and conscience is defiled."[200]

---

[198] Proverbs 3:21-24 (NIV).
[199] Proverbs 2:7 (AMP).
[200] Titus 1:15 (KJV).

Day 104

Solomon	Buddha
If a man pays back evil for good, evil will never leave his house.[201]	[125] If a man offend a harmless, pure, and innocent person, the evil falls back upon that fool, like light dust thrown up against the wind.
A man of perverse heart does not prosper; he whose tongue is deceitful falls into trouble.[202]	

If we offend a pure and harmless person, it will fall back upon us like a dust storm. Paying back evil for good brings trouble down upon us that might never leave us or our home and family.

---

[201] Proverbs 17:13 (NIV).
[202] Proverbs 17:20 (NIV).

Day 105

Solomon

Buddha

The path of life leads upward for the prudent to keep them from going down to the realm of the dead.[203]

Therefore my heart is glad and my glory rejoices; my flesh also will dwell securely. For You will not abandon my soul to Sheol [the abode of the dead or of departed spirits]; nor will You allow Your Holy One to undergo decay. You will make known to me the path of life; in Your presence is fullness of joy; in Your right hand there are pleasures forever.[204]

[126] Some people are born again; evil-doers go to hell; righteous people go to heaven; those who are free from all worldly desires attain Nirvana.

These words of wisdom tell us there is a division after death, resulting in two different destinations. The evil-doers go to hell and are consumed by fire, and the righteous go to heaven and experience joy. Let us be wise and contemplate this.

---

[203] Proverbs 15:24 (NIV).
[204] Psalm 16:9-11 (NASB), a psalm of King David, Solomon's father.

Day 106

Solomon

Buddha

It is better to go to a house of mourning than to go to a house of feasting, for death is the destiny of every man; the living should take this to heart.[205]

No one has power over the spirit to retain the spirit, and no one has power in the day of death. There is no release from that war, and wickedness will not deliver those who are given to it.[206]

127 Not in the sky, not in the midst of the sea, not if we enter into the clefts of the mountains, is there known a spot in the whole world where death could not overcome (the mortal).

128 Not up in the air, nor in the middle of the sea, nor going into a cleft in the mountains—nowhere on earth—is a spot to be found where you could stay and not succumb to death.[207]

There isn't anywhere in the world we can go to hide from death, because death awaits us all. We have no power over it. We cannot contain it, and we will not be discharged from facing it.

---

[205] Ecclesiastes 7:2 (NIV).

[206] Ecclesiastes 8:8 (NKJV).

[207] Dhammapada 128 translated by Thanissaro Bhikkhu, Belief.net, http://www.beliefnet.com/Quotes/Buddhist/Dhammapada/D/Dhammapada-128-Translated-By-Thanissaro-Bhikkhu/Not-Up-In-The-Airnor-In-The-Middle-Of-The-Sea.aspx, retrieved June 5, 2013.

Chapter Ten – Punishment

(Days 107-121, Dhammapada 129-145)

This chapter describes punishment as a universal fear. Even our enemies will live at peace with us if our ways are righteous and we do not punish or kill.

Our anger can act like a punishment to others, just like dealing them a physical blow. A wise man will control his speech and actions, and a gentle answer can dispel another's anger. Being contrary and controlling is like opening the flood gates. It's pretty tough to retrieve the water.

The wicked are punished by their own evil deeds, as if burned by fire, and inflicting pain or punishment on the innocent leads to cruel suffering.

Day 107

Solomon (950 BCE)

The violence of the wicked will destroy them, because they refuse to do justice.[208]

My son, if sinners entice you, do not consent. If they say, "Come with us, let us lie in wait to shed blood; let us lurk secretly for the innocent without cause."[209]

But they lie in wait for their own blood; they ambush their own lives.[210]

Buddha (525 BCE)

[129] All men tremble at punishment, all men fear death; remember that you are like unto them, and do not kill, nor cause slaughter.

[130] All men tremble at punishment, all men love life; remember that thou art like unto them, and do not kill, nor cause slaughter.

In the Ten Commandments given to Moses, God said, "You shall not murder."[211] The first chapter in Proverbs describes at length how those that shed the blood of others, ambush or destroy their own lives. The Buddha said, "Do not kill, nor cause slaughter." And in the Garden of Gethsemane, Jesus said, "Put your sword back in its place . . . for all who draw the sword will die by the sword."[212]

---

[208] Proverbs 21:7 (NKJV).
[209] Proverbs 1:10-11 (NKJV).
[210] Proverbs 1:18 (NASB).
[211] Exodus 20:13 (NIV). Moses lived at least 200 years prior to Solomon.
[212] Matthew 26:52 (NIV).

Day 108

Solomon	Buddha
A man tormented by the guilt of murder will be a fugitive till death; let no one support him.[213]	[131] He who seeking his own happiness punishes or kills beings who also long for happiness, will not find happiness after death.
The violence of the wicked will destroy them, because they refuse to do justice. The way of a guilty man is perverse; but as for the pure, his work is right.[214]	

An extreme form of self-gratification, which results in punishing or killing another human being, will not end in happiness. The result will be acute guilt and loneliness.

Day 109

Solomon	Buddha
When a man's ways are pleasing to the LORD, he makes even his enemies live at peace with him.[215]	[132] He who seeking his own happiness does not punish or kill beings who also long for happiness, will find happiness after death.

If we do not punish or kill and we live a righteous life, even our enemies will live at peace with us.

---

[213] Proverbs 28:17 (NIV).
[214] Proverbs 21:7-8 (NKJV).
[215] Proverbs 16:7 (NIV).

Day 110

Solomon	Buddha
There is one who speaks rashly like the thrusts of a sword, but the tongue of the wise brings healing.[216]	[133] Do not speak harshly to anybody; those who are spoken to will answer thee in the same way. Angry speech is painful, blows for blows will touch thee.
Blessings crown the head of the righteous, but violence overwhelms the mouth of the wicked.[217]	
A gentle answer turns away wrath, but a harsh word stirs up anger.[218]	

When we speak harshly or in anger, it's like dealing someone a physical blow, and we are most often met in kind. A wise man controls his speech, speaking gently with wisdom and kindness. A gentle answer can dispel someone's anger, while a harsh reply inflames it.

---

[216] Proverbs 12:18 (NASB).
[217] Proverbs 10:6 (NIV).
[218] Proverbs 15:1 (NIV).

Day 111

Solomon

It is to a man's honor to avoid strife, but every fool is quick to quarrel.[219]

A hot-tempered man stirs up dissension, but a patient man calms a quarrel.[220]

Starting a quarrel is like breaching a dam; so drop the matter before a dispute breaks out.[221]

Buddha

[134] If, like a shattered metal plate (gong), thou utter not, then thou hast reached Nirvana; contention is not known to thee.

Being contrary and quarreling is like opening the floodgates of a dam. It's pretty tough to retrieve the water. Better to be patient and let a matter drop than to be hot-tempered and regret our speech, which once spoken can turn a minor matter into a major dispute.

[219] Proverbs 20:3 (NIV).
[220] Proverbs 15:18 (NIV).
[221] Proverbs 17:14 (NIV).

Day 112

Solomon

A good name is better than fine perfume, and the day of death better than the day of birth. It is better to go to a house of mourning than to go to a house of feasting, for death is the destiny of every man; the living should take this to heart.[222]

But man, with all his honor and pomp, does not remain; he is like the beasts that perish.[223]

Remember how short my time is; for what futility have You created all the children of men? What man can live and not see death? Can he deliver his life from the power of the grave?[224]

Buddha

[135] As a cowherd with his staff drives his cows into the stable, so do Age and Death drive the life of men.

As the cowboy drives the herd of cattle into a stable, so age drives our lives toward our destiny. Despite our efforts to the contrary, we all will die. We ought to take this to heart and mindfully live out our lives.

---

[222] Ecclesiastes 7:1-2 (NIV).
[223] Psalm 49:12 (AMP), a psalm of King David, Solomon's father.
[224] Psalm 89:47-48 (NKJV).

Day 113

Solomon

The righteousness of the blameless will smooth his way, but the wicked will fall by his own wickedness.[225]

The thing a wicked man fears shall come upon him, but the desire of the [uncompromisingly] righteous shall be granted.[226]

The house of the wicked will be overthrown, but the tent of the upright will flourish.[227]

Buddha

[136] A fool does not know when he commits his evil deeds: but the wicked man burns by his own deeds, as if burnt by fire.

The Buddha makes a distinction between being merely foolish and being wicked. The wicked man is burned by his own deeds. The merely foolish may not even realize they have done something wicked. Far better to live a blameless, righteous life, which makes a smooth, straight path to journey on.

---

[225] Proverbs 11:5 (NASB).
[226] Proverbs 10:24 (AMP).
[227] Proverbs 14:11 (NKJV).

Day 114

Solomon

Buddha

Do not plot harm against your neighbor, who lives trustfully near you. Do not accuse a man for no reason—when he has done you no harm.[228]

[137] He who inflicts pain on innocent and harmless persons, will soon come to one of these ten states: . . . [[138-140]suffering . . . loss . . . injury . . . affliction . . . loss of mind . . . misfortune . . . accusation . . . loss of relations . . . destruction of treasures . . . lightning . . .]

It is disgraceful to plot harm against innocent and harmless people. Let us live peaceably with our neighbors. The apostle Paul wrote to the Romans, "If it is possible, as far as it depends on you, live at peace with everyone."[229]

---

[228] Proverbs 3:29–30 (NIV).
[229] Romans 12:18 (NIV).

Day 115

Solomon	Buddha

He who sows iniquity will reap calamity and futility, and the rod of his wrath [with which he smites others] will fail.[230]

A man is praised according to his wisdom, but men with warped minds are despised.[231]

[137] He who inflicts pain on innocent and harmless persons, will soon come to one of these ten states: . . .

[138] He will have cruel suffering, loss, injury of the body, heavy affliction, or loss of mind.

Inflicting pain or committing a gross injustice to others brings calamity and sufferings upon ourselves, even to the point of warping or losing our minds. Let us walk carefully in our dealings with others.

---

[230] Proverbs 22:8 (AMP).
[231] Proverbs 12:8 (NIV).

Day 116

Solomon

A scoundrel and villain, who goes about with a corrupt mouth, who winks with his eye, signals with his feet and motions with his fingers, who plots evil with deceit in his heart—he always stirs up dissension. Therefore disaster will overtake him in an instant; he will suddenly be destroyed—without remedy.[232]

Buddha

[137] He who inflicts pain on innocent and harmless persons, will soon come to one of these ten states: . . .

[139] Or a misfortune coming from the king, or a fearful accusation, or loss of relations, or destruction of treasures.

Misfortune or calamity from hurting others can descend on us at any time. From accusations to the loss of family or wealth, it can come in a variety of woes. Treating others with consideration and kindness is a wise path.

---

[232] Proverbs 6:12-15 (NIV).

Day 117

Solomon

Buddha

The house of the wicked will be destroyed, but the tent of the upright will flourish.[233] The wicked are overthrown and are no more, but the house of the righteous will stand.[234]

A worthless person, a wicked man, is the one who walks with a perverse mouth, who winks with his eyes, who signals with his feet, who points with his fingers; who with perversity in his heart continually devises evil, who spreads strife. Therefore his calamity will come suddenly; instantly he will be broken and there will be no healing.[235]

[137] He who inflicts pain on innocent and harmless persons, will soon come to one of these ten states: . . .

[140] Or lightning-fire will burn his houses; and when his body is destroyed, the fool will go to hell.

Punishing or inflicting pain on others can lead to our homes being destroyed without warning and even our very lives being taken from us, but the homes of the upright and righteous will stand firm and flourish.

---

[233] Proverbs 14:11 (NASB).
[234] Proverbs 12:7 (NKJV).
[235] Proverbs 6:12-15 (NASB).

Day 118

Solomon

Buddha

Whoever has no rule over his own spirit is like a city broken down, without walls.[236]

I denied myself nothing my eyes desired; I refused my heart no pleasure. My heart took delight in all my work, and this was the reward for all my labor. Yet when I surveyed all that my hands had done and what I had toiled to achieve, everything was meaningless, a chasing after the wind; nothing was gained under the sun.[237]

[141] Not nakedness, not platted hair, not dirt, not fasting, or lying on the earth, not rubbing with dust, not sitting motionless, can purify a mortal who has not overcome desires.

Works do not purify man, and works without any self-control are fruitless. They are like vapor, a chasing after the wind. Restraining our desires and exerting self-control is the better path.

---

[236] Proverbs 25:28 (NKJV).
[237] Ecclesiastes 2:10-11 (NIV).

Day 119

Solomon

Buddha

Who may ascend into the hill of the LORD? Or who may stand in His holy place? He who has clean hands and a pure heart, who has not lifted up his soul to an idol, nor sworn deceitfully. He shall receive blessing from the LORD, and righteousness from the God of his salvation.[238]

He who loves a pure heart and whose speech is gracious will have the king for his friend.[239]

[142] He who, though dressed in fine apparel, exercises tranquillity [sic], is quiet, subdued, restrained, chaste, and has ceased to find fault with all other beings, he indeed is a Brahmana, an ascetic (sramana), a friar (bhikshu).

What is of lasting value, is not our outward appearance or wearing of fine apparel, but the conduct and qualities of the inward man. Restrained and chaste, non-judgmental, with hands that have not done harm and a pure heart, let us strive to lead a meditative, simple life.

---

[238] Psalm 24:3-5 (NKJV), a psalm of King David, Solomon's father.
[239] Proverbs 22:11 (NIV).

Day 120

Solomon

Buddha

Do not be like the horse or
the mule, which have no
understanding but must be
controlled by bit and bridle
or they will not come to
you.[240]

[143] Is there in this world any
man so restrained by
humility that he does not
mind reproof, as a well-
trained horse the whip?

[144] Like a well-trained horse
when touched by the whip,
be ye active and lively, and
by faith, by virtue, by
energy, by meditation, by
discernment of the law you
will overcome this great
pain (of reproof), perfect in
knowledge and in behaviour
[*sic*], and never forgetful.

Pride can hold us back from receiving a deserved reproof. Let
us not be like a wild horse that has to be beaten to submit, but
rather let us be rich in humility and guide ourselves with constant
small corrections, like the rider gently guiding the well-behaved
horse.

---

[240] Psalm 32:9 (NIV), a psalm of King David, Solomon's father.

Day 121

Solomon

He is on the path of life who heeds instruction, but he who ignores reproof goes astray.[241]

He who disdains instruction despises his own soul, but he who heeds rebuke gets understanding.[242]

Buddha

[145] Well-makers lead the water (wherever they like); fletchers bend the arrow; carpenters bend a log of wood; good people fashion themselves.

As an expert carpenter bends wood to build a find house, so we ought to fashion ourselves. Seeking the truth and not letting go of it. Getting wisdom, discipline and understanding. We can use these tools to change our lives.

---

[241] Proverbs 10:17 (NASB).
[242] Proverbs 15:32 (NKJV).

Chapter Eleven – Old Age

(Days 122-129, Dhammapada 146-156)

This chapter focuses on the aging of our bodies and the consequences of our actions over a lifetime. Some actions can even lead to premature death, such as envy, pride and deceit.

Beware the weariness of the cycle of life. Discipline and self-control are the first steps to obtaining wisdom and understanding, and wisdom is to be held in the highest value.

If we have not obtained good instruction in our youth, it is up to us to discipline ourselves, otherwise, we will go astray and pay for the consequences of our actions.

Day 122

Solomon (950 BCE)

Buddha (525 BCE)

And I saw that wisdom excels folly as light excels darkness.[243]

[146] How is there laughter, how is there joy, as this world is always burning? Why do you not seek a light, ye who are surrounded by darkness?

You save the humble but bring low those whose eyes are haughty. You, O LORD, keep my lamp burning; my God turns my darkness into light.[244]

Wealth and riches are in his house, and his righteousness endures forever. Even in darkness light dawns for the upright, for the gracious and compassionate and righteous man.[245]

Light is better than darkness. Knowledge is better than ignorance. Why suffer in darkness? Seek the light. Seek wisdom and knowledge.

---

[243] Ecclesiastes 2:13 (NASB).
[244] Psalm 18:27-28 (NIV), a psalm of King David, Solomon's father.
[245] Psalm 112:3-4 (NIV).

Day 123

Solomon	**Buddha**

My wounds fester and are loathsome because of my sinful folly. I am bowed down and brought very low; all day long I go about mourning. My back is filled with searing pain; there is no health in my body. I am feeble and utterly crushed; I groan in anguish of heart.[246]

[147] Look at this dressed-up lump, covered with wounds, joined together, sickly, full of many thoughts, which has no strength, no hold!

Better to go to the house of mourning than to go to the house of feasting, for that is the end of all men; and the living will take it to heart.[247]

[148] This body is wasted, full of sickness, and frail; this heap of corruption breaks to pieces, life indeed ends in death.

Our bodies can be a source of great suffering. Whether brought on by our own evil, selfish actions, or by others acting selfishly or with evil intent, we can suffer until we have no more strength. Our bodies are transitory, and death awaits each of us.

---

[246] Psalm 38:5-8 (NIV), a psalm of King David, Solomon's father.
[247] Ecclesiastes 7:2 (NKJV).

Day 124

Solomon	**Buddha**
A heart at peace gives life to the body, but envy rots the bones.[248]	[149] Those white bones, like gourds thrown away in the autumn, what pleasure is there in looking at them?
A proud and haughty man—"Scoffer" is his name; he acts with arrogant pride.[249]	[150] After a stronghold has been made of the bones, it is covered with flesh and blood, and there dwell in it old age and death, pride and deceit.

What pleasure is there in looking at old dried up bones? It only reminds us that we will all face death. Let us avoid envy, pride and deceit, as it will hasten the end of our life.

---

[248] Proverbs 14:30 (NIV).
[249] Proverbs 21:24 (NKJV).

Day 125

Solomon

The desire of the [consistently] righteous brings only good, but the expectation of the wicked brings wrath.[250]

The wages of the righteous is life, but the earnings of the wicked are sin and death.[251]

The path of life leads upward for the prudent to keep them from going down to the realm of the dead.[252]

Buddha

[151] The brilliant chariots of kings are destroyed, the body also approaches destruction, but the virtue of good people never approaches destruction,— thus do the good say to the good.

Our bodies will be destroyed, but the good we do lives on. What a great motivation that is to doing good!

---

[250] Proverbs 11:23 (AMP).
[251] Proverbs 10:16 (NIV).
[252] Proverbs 15:24 (NIV).

Day 126

Solomon

Leave the presence of a fool, or you will not discern words of knowledge. The wisdom of the sensible is to understand his way, but the foolishness of fools is deceit.[253]

The simple inherit folly, but the prudent are crowned with knowledge.[254]

Buddha

[152] A man who has learnt little, grows old like an ox; his flesh grows, but his knowledge does not grow.

The mind of an ignorant fool does not contain knowledge, and spending time with him will not bring to light any wisdom from his speech. Better to leave him and seek wisdom, or you will cease to recognize it.

---

[253] Proverbs 14:7-8 (NASB).
[254] Proverbs 14:18 (NKJV).

Day 127

Solomon

Buddha

All things are wearisome; man is not able to tell it. The eye is not satisfied with seeing, nor is the ear filled with hearing. That which has been is that which will be, and that which has been done is that which will be done. So there is nothing new under the sun.[255]

Whatever is has already been, and what will be has been before; and God will call the past to account.[256]

[153, 154.] Looking for the maker of this tabernacle, I shall have to run through a course of many births, so long as I do not find (him); and painful is birth again and again. But now, maker of the tabernacle, thou hast been seen; thou shalt not make up this tabernacle again. All thy rafters are broken, thy ridge-pole is sundered; the mind, approaching the Eternal (visankhara, nirvana), has attained to the extinction of all desires.

The writings above speak of an awareness of and weariness with the cycle of life.

---

[255] Ecclesiastes 1:8-9 (NASB).
[256] Ecclesiastes 3:15 (NIV).

Day 128

Solomon	Buddha
He who ignores discipline despises himself, but whoever heeds correction gains understanding.[257]	[155] Men who have not observed proper discipline, and have not gained treasure in their youth, perish like old herons in a lake without fish.
Buy the truth and do not sell it; get wisdom, discipline and understanding.[258]	

Discipline and self-control are the first steps to obtaining wisdom and understanding, and wisdom is to be held in the highest value. Solomon wrote, "For wisdom is more precious than rubies, and nothing you desire can compare with her."[259]

---

[257] Proverbs 15:32 (NIV).
[258] Proverbs 23:23 (NIV).
[259] Proverbs 8:11 (NIV).

Day 129

Solomon

For your ways are in full view of the LORD, and he examines all your paths. The evil deeds of the wicked ensnare them; the cords of their sins hold them fast. For lack of discipline they will die, led astray by their own great folly.[260]

Buddha

[156] Men who have not observed proper discipline, and have not gained treasure in their youth, lie, like broken bows, sighing after the past.

In our youth, if we have not received proper instruction, and in turn if we do not discipline ourselves, we will get enmeshed in our sins. We will go astray and will have to pay for the consequences of our actions.

---

[260] Proverbs 5:21-23 (NIV).

Chapter Twelve – Self

(Days 130-138, Dhammapada 157-166)

Chapter Twelve discusses the need to direct and teach ourselves, and subdue our desires, while being uncompromising about choosing to live a wise and righteous life.

It is important to avoid doing evil and committing bad deeds. Wicked actions can choke the life out of us. We ought to be consistently pruning evil out of our lives, and purifying ourselves of any evil conduct, thereby avoiding its consequences.

Day 130

Solomon (950 BCE)

The highway of the upright avoids evil; he who guards his way guards his life.[261]

Blessed (happy, fortunate, to be envied) is the man who listens to me [wise instruction], watching daily at my gates, waiting at the posts of my doors.[262]

Buddha (525 BCE)

[157] If a man hold himself dear, let him watch himself carefully; during one at least out of the three watches a wise man should be watchful.

By holding ourselves dear, being watchful, avoiding evil, and keeping wise instruction before us, all these help us to guard our lives and keep us walking on a blessed path.

---

[261] Proverbs 16:17 (NIV).
[262] Proverbs 8:34 (AMP).

Day 131

Solomon	Buddha
Give instruction to a wise man and he will be yet wiser; teach a righteous man (one upright and in right standing with God) and he will increase in learning.[263] The teaching of the wise is a fountain of life, to turn aside from the snares of death. [264]	[158] Let each man direct himself first to what is proper, then let him teach others; thus a wise man will not suffer.

Teach a wise man, he becomes wiser still and avoids the suffering of folly. We cannot impart wisdom to others, unless we first train up ourselves.

---

[263] Proverbs 9:9 (AMP).
[264] Proverbs 13:14 (NASB).

Day 132

Solomon	Buddha
The simple believes every word, but the prudent considers well his steps.[265] Hear, my son, and be wise. And guide your heart in the way. . . .[266]	[159] If a man make himself as he teaches others to be, then, being himself well subdued, he may subdue (others); one's own self is indeed difficult to subdue.

Being king, Solomon had no human authority to report to, so he reported directly to himself, just as Buddha advocated doing, and he exhorted his sons to do likewise.

Day 133

Solomon	Buddha
The [uncompromisingly] righteous is delivered out of trouble, and the wicked gets into it instead.[267]	[160] Self is the lord of self, who else could be the lord? With self well subdued, a man finds a lord such as few can find.

Subduing self and being uncompromising about wise and righteous living delivers us out of trouble. The alternative is to live wickedly and get into trouble without fail.

---

[265] Proverbs 14:15 (NKJV).
[266] Proverbs 23:19 (NIV).
[267] Proverbs 11:8 (AMP).

Day 134

Solomon

They will eat the fruit of their ways and be filled with the fruit of their schemes. For the waywardness of the simple will kill them, and the complacency of fools will destroy them.[268]

Penalties are prepared for mockers, and beatings for the backs of fools.[269]

A whip for the horse, a bridle for the donkey, and a rod for the fool's back.[270]

Buddha

[161] The evil done by oneself, self-begotten, self-bred, crushes the foolish, as a diamond breaks a precious stone.

The evil we do comes back upon us. Whatever schemes we might devise, whatever ill we might perpetrate, it will always come to fruition and see the light of day. Then we will pay in one form or another for the harm we have caused.

---

[268] Proverbs 1:31-32 (NIV).
[269] Proverbs 19:29 (NIV).
[270] Proverbs 26:3 (NKJV).

Day 135

Solomon

His own iniquities entrap the wicked man, and he is caught in the cords of his sin.[271]

Do not those who plot evil go astray? But those who plan what is good find love and faithfulness.[272]

Buddha

[162] He whose wickedness is very great brings himself down to that state where his enemy wishes him to be, as a creeper does with the tree which it surrounds.

[163] Bad deeds, and deeds hurtful to ourselves, are easy to do; what is beneficial and good, that is very difficult to do.

As an ivy can choke out any plant life in its path, we are choked out and entrapped by our own wicked actions, and our enemies delight in it. We do not need to fear disaster when we do what is beneficial and good.

---

[271] Proverbs 5:22 (NKJV).
[272] Proverbs 14:22 (NIV).

Day 136

Solomon

Buddha

Do not speak to a fool, for he will scorn the wisdom of your words.[273]

He who scorns instruction will pay for it. . . .[274]

. . . the wicked will fall by his own wickedness.[275]

[164] The foolish man who scorns the rule of the venerable (Arahat), of the elect (Ariya), of the virtuous, and follows false doctrine, he bears fruit to his own destruction, like the fruits of the Katthaka reed.

Scorn, contempt and ridicule for wisdom and instruction is foolish and will breed consequences. The fool's disdain for wisdom results in calamity and destruction.

---

[273] Proverbs 23:9 (NIV).
[274] Proverbs 13:13a (NIV).
[275] Proverbs 11:5b (NKJV).

Day 137

Solomon	Buddha

Who can say, I have made my heart clean, I am pure from my sin? Diverse weights [one for buying and another for selling] and diverse measures—both of them are exceedingly offensive and abhorrent to the Lord. Even a child is known by his acts, whether [or not] what he does is pure and right.[276]

The righteousness of the blameless makes a straight way for them, but the wicked are brought down by their own wickedness.[277]

[165] By oneself the evil is done, by oneself one suffers; by oneself evil is left undone, by oneself one is purified. Purity and impurity belong to oneself, no one can purify another.

Even in young children, we recognize whether what they do is pure and right. We need to recognize that in ourselves. Our behavior can be pure or impure, good or evil. We need to be aware of our behavior and purify ourselves of evil conduct and avoid its consequences.

---

[276] Proverbs 20:9-11 (AMP).
[277] Proverbs 11:5 (NIV).

Day 138

Solomon

Buddha

He who earnestly seeks after and craves righteousness, mercy, and loving-kindness will find life in addition to righteousness . . . and honor.[278]

[166] Let no one forget his own duty for the sake of another's, however great; let a man, after he has discerned his own duty, be always attentive to his duty.

He who obeys instructions guards his life, but he who is contemptuous of his ways will die.[279]

We ought to be mindful that taking care of our responsibilities is part of living a righteous life. As we earnestly seek after wisdom and righteousness, let us also fulfill our duties. If we scorn instruction and wisdom, and do not fulfill our duties, the results could cost us our lives.

---

[278] Proverbs 21:21 (AMP).
[279] Proverbs 19:16 (NIV).

Chapter Thirteen – The World

(Days 139-149, Dhammapada 167-178)

This chapter expounds on the temptation of the world, and how the world is not to be our focus. We can choose evil, we can live thoughtlessly, we can follow a false teaching and be a friend of the world, or we can choose wisdom and be thoughtful and mindful of our ways.

Wisdom and moral excellence are more precious than a wealth of jewels. All the world has to offer is of no use to us without wisdom. Let us value wisdom above wealth, and knowledge above the fleeting glitter of the world.

Day 139

Solomon (950 BCE)

Her feet go down to death; her steps lead straight to the grave. She gives no thought to the way of life; her paths are crooked, but she knows it not.[280]

A wicked man puts on the bold, unfeeling face [of guilt], but as for the upright, he considers, directs, and establishes his way [with the confidence of integrity].[281]

Buddha (525 BCE)

[167] Do not follow the evil law! Do not live on in thoughtlessness! Do not follow false doctrine! Be not a friend of the world.

Though the first verse above speaks of an adulteress, however, it is applicable to anyone who chooses an evil path. We all have a choice. We can choose evil, we can live thoughtlessly, we can follow a false teaching and be a friend of the world, or we can choose wisdom and be thoughtful and mindful of our ways.

---

[280] Proverbs 5:5-6 (NIV).
[281] Proverbs 21:29 (AMP).

Day 140

Solomon

Buddha

In the way of righteousness there is life; along that path is immortality.[282]

The prospect of the righteous is joy. . . .[283]

But the path of the just is like the shining sun, that shines ever brighter unto the perfect day.[284]

[168] Rouse thyself! do not be idle! Follow the law of virtue! The virtuous rests in bliss in this world and in the next.

As we follow the law of virtue, we find life and joy, and our path shines like the sun. Let us not be idle. Let us be roused to walk the path of righteousness and rest in its bliss.

---

[282] Proverbs 12:28 (NIV).
[283] Proverbs 10:28a (NIV).
[284] Proverbs 4:18 (NKJV).

Day 141

Solomon

Happy is the man who finds wisdom, and the man who gains understanding; for her proceeds are better than the profits of silver, and her gain than fine gold. She is more precious than rubies, and all the things you may desire cannot compare with her. Length of days is in her right hand, in her left hand riches and honor. Her ways are ways of pleasantness, and all her paths are peace. She is a tree of life to those who take hold of her, and happy are all who retain her.[285]

Buddha

[169] Follow the law of virtue; do not follow that of sin. The virtuous rests in bliss in this world and in the next.

Following after wisdom, moral excellence, goodness and righteousness is more precious and profitable than a wealth of jewels. Nothing we might desire is more valuable.

---

[285] Proverbs 3:13-18 (NKJV).

Day 142

Solomon

Buddha

"Meaningless! Meaningless!" says the Teacher. "Utterly meaningless! Everything is meaningless."[286]

[170] Look upon the world as a bubble, look upon it as a mirage: the king of death does not see him who thus looks down upon the world.

The Hebrew word translated as "meaningless" in the New International Version appears differently in other Bible translations as "vanity", "vapors", or "smoke". We do well to acknowledge the transient nature of life.

---

[286] Ecclesiastes 1:2 (NIV).

Day 143

Solomon

Buddha

Better is a poor and wise youth than an old and foolish king who no longer knows how to receive counsel (friendly reproof and warning).[287]

[171] Come, look at this glittering world, like unto a royal chariot; the foolish are immersed in it, but the wise do not touch it.

Better is a little with righteousness, than vast revenues without justice.[288]

What use is all the world has to offer without wisdom? It is worse to be a wealthy, foolish king than to be a poor, wise youth. Let us value wisdom above wealth, and knowledge above the fleeting, glitter of the world.

---

[287] Ecclesiastes 4:13 (AMP).
[288] Proverbs 16:8 (NKJV).

Day 144

Solomon	Buddha

Whoever disregards discipline comes to poverty and shame, but whoever heeds correction is honored. [289]

[172] He who formerly was reckless and afterwards became sober, brightens up this world, like the moon when freed from clouds.

Reckless words pierce like a sword, but the tongue of the wise brings healing.[290]

Reckless actions and words are dangerous to ourselves and those around us. When we give up reckless behavior and begin to live a self-controlled life, it brings healing and light into our life and positively affects those around us.

---

[289] Proverbs 13:18 (NIV).
[290] Proverbs 12:18 (NIV).

Day 145

Solomon

Buddha

Hatred stirs up strife, but love covers all sins.[291]
The evil will bow down before the good, and the wicked at the gates of the righteous.[292]

Do they not go astray who devise evil? But mercy and truth belong to those who devise good.[293]

[173] He whose evil deeds are covered by good deeds, brightens up this world, like the moon when freed from clouds.

Love covers sins. Good deeds cover evil deeds. The evil will bow before the good. The Apostle Peter wrote, "Above all, love each other deeply, because love covers over a multitude of sins."[294]

---

[291] Proverbs 10:12 (NKJV).
[292] Proverbs 14:19 (NASB).
[293] Proverbs 14:22 (NKJV).
[294] 1 Peter 4:8 (NIV).

Day 146

Solomon

Then I saw that wisdom excels folly as light excels darkness. The wise man's eyes are in his head, but the fool walks in darkness. Yet I myself perceived that the same event happens to them all.[295]

For the wise man, like the fool, will not be long remembered; in days to come both will be forgotten. Like the fool, the wise man too must die![296]

Who may ascend the hill of the LORD? Who may stand in his holy place? He who has clean hands and a pure heart, who does not lift up his soul to an idol or swear by what is false.[297]

Buddha

[174] This world is dark, few only can see here; a few only go to heaven, like birds escaped from the net.

[175] The swans go on the path of the sun, they go through the ether by means of their miraculous power; the wise are led out of this world, when they have conquered Mara and his train.

Life often is complicated and doesn't seem very black and white, but we can choose to see through the darkness to the light, rather than living foolishly in the dark. Walking in wisdom, and having clean hands and a pure heart, prepares us to leave this world in good conscience, like a bird released from a net.

---

[295] Ecclesiastes 2:13-14 (NKJV).
[296] Ecclesiastes 2:16 (NIV).
[297] Psalm 24:3-4 (NIV), a psalm of King David, Solomon's father.

155

Day 147

Solomon

Wisdom will save you from the ways of wicked men, from men whose words are perverse, who leave the straight paths to walk in dark ways, who delight in doing wrong and rejoice in the perverseness of evil, whose paths are crooked and who are devious in their ways.[298]

Buddha

[176] If a man has transgressed one law, and speaks lies, and scoffs at another world, there is no evil he will not do.

Lying often leads to other evil deeds. Wisdom is the cure. If we guard our thoughts, our speech, and our actions with wisdom, we will be spared the consequences of allowing evil into our lives.

Day 148

Solomon

One man gives freely, yet gains even more. Another man withholds unduly, but comes to poverty.[299]

Buddha

[177] The uncharitable do not go to the world of the gods; fools only do not praise liberality; a wise man rejoices in liberality, and through it becomes blessed in the other world.

It is foolish to be miserly, and to withhold even when it is just to give. Generosity brings blessing into our lives in this life and the next. If we are wise, we will rejoice in giving liberally.

---

[298] Proverbs 2:12-15 (NIV).
[299] Proverbs 11:24 (NIV).

Day 149

Solomon	Buddha
Better is a little with righteousness than great income with injustice.[300] How much better is it to get wisdom than gold! Yea, to get understanding is rather to be chosen than silver.[301]	[178] Better than sovereignty over the earth, better than going to heaven, better than lordship over all worlds, is the reward of the first step in holiness.

Of what use if power or wealth without holiness or righteousness? Better to take a single step toward righteousness, than be enticed by all the world might offer. Jesus said, "For what profit is it to a man if he gains the whole world, and loses his own soul?"[302]

---

[300] Proverbs 16:8 (NASB).
[301] Proverbs 16:16 (ASV).
[302] Matthew 16:26a (NKJV).

Chapter Fourteen – The Buddha

(The Awakened)

(Days 150-164, Dhammapada 179-196)

This chapter describes aspects of the awakened (the Buddha). Through self-control and restraint, we can avoid many pitfalls in life. If we purify our minds and choose to do good during our lifetime, this is a path to awakening our minds to all that is truthful.

Having patience, being slow to anger, avoiding strife, forgiving offences, each of these is driven by self-control, for without it we are lost to our baser instincts. Awakening requires moderation, self-control, and meditation on the law, not the willful pursuit of pleasure.

Blessed, happy and fortunate are those who seek after wisdom, who pursue it daily, who are devoted to it, and put it into practice.

Day 150

Solomon (950 BCE)

My son, preserve sound judgment and discernment, do not let them out of your sight; they will be life for you, an ornament to grace your neck. Then you will go on your way in safety, and your foot will not stumble; when you lie down, you will not be afraid; when you lie down, your sleep will be sweet. Have no fear of sudden disaster or of the ruin that overtakes the wicked, for the LORD will be your confidence and will keep your foot from being snared.[303]

Buddha (525 BCE)

[179] He whose conquest is not conquered again, into whose conquest no one in this world enters, by what track can you lead him, the Awakened, the Omniscient, the trackless?

When we preserve sound judgment and discernment, when we make knowledge and wisdom a priority, we will avoid walking down the wrong or evil path (track). We will not be snared by desires. We can go our way in safety and sleep peacefully. The sudden disaster that overtakes the wicked will not come to our door.

---

[303] Proverbs 3:21-26 (NIV).

Day 151

Solomon

Buddha

In the paths of the wicked lie thorns and snares, but he who guards his soul stays far from them.[304]

[180] He whom no desire with its snares and poisons can lead astray, by what track can you lead him, the Awakened, the Omniscient, the trackless?

Through self-control and restraint, we can avoid many snared and pitfalls in life. We ought to guard our soul and avoid evil.

---

[304] Proverbs 22:5 (NIV).

Day 152

Solomon	Buddha

Blessed is the man who walks not in the counsel of the ungodly, nor stands in the path of sinners, nor sits in the seat of the scornful; but his delight is in the law of the Lord, and in His law he meditates day and night. He shall be like a tree planted by the rivers of water, that brings forth its fruit in its season, whose leaf also shall not wither; and whatever he does shall prosper.[305]

[181] Even the gods envy those who are awakened and not forgetful, who are given to meditation, who are wise, and who delight in the repose of retirement (from the world).

If we are wise, we will avoid seeking the counsel of the wicked, and will meditate on the law. Meditation on the law, on truth, and on wisdom, causes us to flourish like a tree planted by water. Even "the gods" will envy us as we awaken to wisdom.

---

[305] Psalm 1:1–3 (NKJV), a psalm of King David, Solomon's father.

Day 153

Solomon	Buddha
So I hated life, because the work that is done under the sun was grievous to me. All of it is meaningless, a chasing after the wind. . . . What does a man get for all the toil and anxious striving with which he labors under the sun? All his days his work is pain and grief; even at night his mind does not rest. This too is meaningless.[306]	[182] Difficult (to obtain) is the conception of men, difficult is the life of mortals, difficult is the hearing of the True Law, difficult is the birth of the Awakened (the attainment of Buddhahood).

Life is difficult. We work, we struggle, our bodies wear out and don't serve us as we wish they would. Just as Solomon wrote, some days it seems all very meaningless. What does give meaning to our lives is pursuing wisdom and righteousness. Hearing the true law and being awakened to it.

---

[306] Ecclesiastes 2:17, 22-23 (NIV).

Day 154

Solomon	Buddha
Do they not go astray who devise evil? But mercy and truth belong to those who devise good.[307]	[183] Not to commit any sin, to do good, and to purify one's mind, that is the teaching of (all) the Awakened.
I know that there is nothing better for men than to be happy and do good while they live.[308]	

Devising evil and committing sin, these lead us astray, but if we purify our minds and choose to do good during our lifetime, there is no better path to awakening our minds to all that is truthful.

---

[307] Proverbs 14:22 (NKJV).
[308] Ecclesiastes 3:12 (NIV).

Day 155

Solomon

It is a man's honor to avoid strife, but every fool is quick to quarrel.[309]

He who conceals a transgression seeks love, but he who repeats a matter separates intimate friends.[310]

He who is slow to anger is better than the mighty. And he who rules his spirit than he who takes a city.[311]

Buddha

[184] The Awakened call patience the highest penance, long-suffering the highest Nirvana; for he is not an anchorite (pravragita) who strikes others, he is not an ascetic (sramana) who insults others.

Having patience, being slow to anger, avoiding strife, quarreling and violence, forgiving offenses, all these are a calling, a way of life to those who seek after wisdom and truth. Each is driven by self-control, for without it we are lost to our baser instincts.

---

[309] Proverbs 20:3 (NIV).
[310] Proverbs 17:9 (NASB).
[311] Proverbs 16:32 (NKJV).

Day 156

Solomon

Two things have I required of thee; deny me them not before I die: Remove far from me vanity and lies: give me neither poverty nor riches; feed me with food convenient for me: Lest I be full, and deny thee, and say, Who is the LORD? or lest I be poor, and steal, and take the name of my God in vain.[312]

Do not be overrighteous, neither be overwise—why destroy yourself? Do not be overwicked, and do not be a fool—why die before your time? It is good to grasp the one and not let go of the other. The man who fears God will avoid all extremes.[313]

Buddha

[185] Not to blame, not to strike, to live restrained under the law, to be moderate in eating, to sleep and sit alone, and to dwell on the highest thoughts,— this is the teaching of the Awakened.

The world encourages us to excess in every area of our lives. In restraining ourselves, in choosing moderation, we may appear like we are making a great sacrifice to our friends and family, but in moderation we keep alive gratitude. Rather than filling our minds and stomachs with the things of this world, we can meditate on the highest and best thoughts.

---

[312] Proverbs 30:7-9 (KJV). Proverbs 30 is attributed to Agur, son of Jakeh.
[313] Ecclesiastes 7:16-18 (NIV).

Day 157

Solomon

Buddha

My son, observe the commandment of your father and do not forsake the teaching of your mother; bind them continually on your heart; tie them around your neck. . . . Do not desire her beauty* in your heart, nor let her capture you with her eyelids. For on account of a harlot one is reduced to a loaf of bread, and an adulteress hunts for the precious life. Can a man take fire in his bosom and his clothes not be burned? Or can a man walk on hot coals and his feet not be scorched? So is the one who goes in to his neighbor's wife; whoever touches her will not go unpunished.[314]

[196] There is no satisfying lusts, even by a shower of gold pieces; he who knows that lusts have a short taste and cause pain, he is wise.

*Referring to the evil woman, the adulteress.

Lusting and coveting are insatiable desires and cannot be bought off. At the same time, when pursued they are fleeting, temporal, and they lead to pain and punishment. Meditating on and keeping the law in our hearts and minds saves us from causing pain to ourselves and others.

---

[314] Proverbs 6:20-21, 25-29 (NASB).

Day 158

Solomon

I thought in my heart, "Come now, I will test you with pleasure to find out what is good." But that also proved to be meaningless. "Laughter," I said, "is foolish. And what does pleasure accomplish?"[315]

The heart of the wise is in the house of mourning, but the heart of fools is in the house of pleasure.[316]

Buddha

[187] Even in heavenly pleasures he finds no satisfaction, the disciple who is fully awakened delights only in the destruction of all desires.

A devotion to pleasure, believing that pleasure is the highest good, that is hedonism. Just as lust is fleeting, so pleasure is fleeting. Finding lasting satisfaction requires moderation, self-control, and meditation on the law, not the willful pursuit of pleasure.

---

[315] Ecclesiastes 2:1-2 (NIV).
[316] Ecclesiastes 7:4 (NIV).

Day 159

Solomon

My son, let them not vanish from your sight; keep sound wisdom and discretion, so they will be life to your soul and adornment to your neck. Then you will walk in your way securely and your foot will not stumble. When you lie down, you will not be afraid; when you lie down, your sleep will be sweet. Do not be afraid of sudden fear nor of the onslaught of the wicked when it comes; for the LORD will be your confidence and will keep your foot from being caught.[317]

Buddha

[188] Men, driven by fear, go to many a refuge, to mountains and forests, to groves and sacred trees.

[189] But that is not a safe refuge, that is not the best refuge; a man is not delivered from all pains after having gone to that refuge.

If we allow fear to drive us, we will seek out any refuge we can find that will give us a moment's peace of mind. Wisdom is the best refuge, keeping us safe from pain and the snares of evil behavior.

---

[317] Proverbs 3:21-26 (NASB).

Day 160

Solomon	Buddha
Every word of God is flawless; he is a shield to those who take refuge in him.[318]	[190] He who takes refuge with Buddha, the Law, and the Church; he who, with clear understanding, sees the four holy truths:—
He who fears the LORD has a secure fortress, and for his children it will be a refuge.[319]	[192] That is the safe refuge, that is the best refuge; having gone to that refuge, a man is delivered from all pain.

If we value and meditate on the law and wisdom, and live according to all we have learned, we find refuge. Doing so, we become an example to our children, and if they in turn follow suit, they find refuge as well.

---

[318] Proverbs 30:5 (NIV). Proverbs 30 is attributed to Agur, son of Jakeh.
[319] Proverbs 14:26 (NIV).

Day 161

Solomon

For all his days are but pain and sorrow, and his work is a vexation and grief; his mind takes no rest even at night. This is also vanity (emptiness, falsity, and futility)![320]

The way of the LORD is a refuge for the righteous, but it is the ruin of those who do evil.[321]

A prudent man sees danger and takes refuge, but the simple keep going and suffer for it.[322]

Buddha

[190b] He who, with clear understanding, sees the four holy truths:—

[191] Viz. pain, the origin of pain, the destruction of pain, and the eightfold holy way that leads to the quieting of pain;—

[192] That is the safe refuge, that is the best refuge; having gone to that refuge, a man is delivered from all pain.

If all we do is walk selfishly and mindlessly through life, pain will plague us, even to the point of disrupting our sleep. When we walk mindfully in holiness and righteousness, that holy way leads to less pain. If we are prudent, we will seek refuge in the law, if not, we will suffer for it.

---

[320] Ecclesiastes 2:23 (AMP).
[321] Proverbs 10:29 (NIV).
[322] Proverbs 22:3 (NIV).

Day 162

Solomon

When the righteous prosper, the city rejoices. . . .[323]

Buddha

[193] A supernatural person (a Buddha) is not easily found, he is not born everywhere. Wherever such a sage is born, that race prospers.

Wherever a righteous person dwells, those around him rejoice and prosper as well. As we pursue righteousness, we will find it overflowing onto those around us and blessing them.

---

[323] Proverbs 11:10a (NIV).

Day 163

Solomon

Buddha

Now therefore listen to me [Wisdom], O you sons; for blessed (happy, fortunate, to be envied) are those who keep my ways. Hear instruction and be wise, and do not refuse or neglect it. Blessed (happy, fortunate, to be envied) is the man who listens to me, watching daily at my gates, waiting at the posts of my doors. For whoever finds me [Wisdom] finds life and draws forth and obtains favor from the Lord.[324]

[194] Happy is the arising of the awakened, happy is the teaching of the True Law, happy is peace in the church, happy is the devotion of those who are at peace.

Blessed, happy, fortunate, and to be envied are those who seek after wisdom, who pursue it daily, who are devoted to it, who hear good, wise instruction and are receptive and put it into practice. For when we find wisdom, we find life and peace.

---

[324] Proverbs 8:32-35 (AMP).

Day 164

Solomon

A good name is more desirable than great riches; to be esteemed is better than silver or gold.[325]

Buddha

[195, 196.] He who pays homage to those who deserve homage, whether the awakened (Buddha) or their disciples, those who have overcome the host (of evils), and crossed the flood of sorrow, he who pays homage to such as have found deliverance and know no fear, his merit can never be measured by anybody.

A fine reputation is more valuable than great riches. When we pay homage to someone, when we do something or give something to them in recognition of their worth, attainments and integrity, we are expressing our recognition of their merits. We embrace those attributes as something we honor, and, by extension, that we wish to attain as well.

---

[325] Proverbs 22:1 (NIV).

Chapter Fifteen – Happiness

(Days 165-175, Dhammapada 197-208)

Chapter Fifteen focuses on happiness. Being happy is healing for our bodies and may even prevent illness.

Happiness is being free from hate, free from greed, free from the burdens of material belongings, free from passions and desires, and free to be content and joyful.

There is virtue and happiness in both companionship and solitude.

Day 165

Solomon (950 BCE)

I know that there is nothing better for men than to be happy and do good while they live.[326]

If your enemy is hungry, give him food to eat; and if he is thirsty, give him water to drink.[327]

A happy heart is good medicine and a cheerful mind works healing, but a broken spirit dries up the bones.[328]

Buddha (525 BCE)

[197] Let us live happily then, not hating those who hate us! among men who hate us let us dwell free from hatred!

[198] Let us live happily then, free from ailments among the ailing! among men who are ailing let us dwell free from ailments!

If we spend our lives doing good and being happy, we have no time for hatred. In not hating those who hate us, we can go a step further and do good to them. Solomon encouraged the giving of food and beverage to an enemy as an act of love and goodness. Being happy is healing for our bodies, and may even prevent illness.

---

[326] Ecclesiastes 3:12 (NIV).
[327] Proverbs 25:21 (NASB).
[328] Proverbs 17:22 (AMP).

Day 166

Solomon	**Buddha**

He who is greedy for gain troubles his own house, but he who hates bribes will live.[329]

A greedy man stirs up dissension, but he who trusts in the LORD will prosper.[330]

[199] Let us live happily then, free from greed among the greedy! among men who are greedy let us dwell free from greed!

Part of being happy is being free from greed, and not being influenced by another's greed. Greed only brings trouble to ourselves and our families. It creates conflict, quarrels and discord, and if we try to hide it, it can create distrust in relationships.

---

[329] Proverbs 15:27 (NKJV).
[330] Proverbs 28:25 (NIV).

Day 167

Solomon

Better is the little that the [uncompromisingly] righteous have than the abundance [of possessions] of many who are wrong and wicked.[331]

Two things I ask of you, O LORD; do not refuse me before I die: keep falsehood and lies far from me; give me neither poverty nor riches, but give me only my daily bread. Otherwise, I may have too much and disown you and say, 'Who is the LORD?' Or I may become poor and steal, and so dishonor the name of my God.[332]

Buddha

[200] Let us live happily then, though we call nothing our own! We shall be like the bright gods, feeding on happiness!

Contentment with moderation is a happy state. Better to have little and be happy than great wealth with wickedness and evil creeping into our lives.

---

[331] Psalm 37:16 (AMP), a psalm of King David, Solomon's father.
[332] Proverbs 30:7-9 (NIV). Proverbs 30 is attributed to Agur, son of Jakeh.

Day 168

Solomon

He holds victory in store for the upright, he is a shield to those whose walk is blameless.[333]

For lack of guidance a nation falls, but many advisers make victory sure.[334]

Buddha

[201] Victory breeds hatred, for the conquered is unhappy. He who has given up both victory and defeat, he, the contented, is happy.

While Solomon, who ruled over a peaceful kingdom, focused on achieving victory by being upright and having many advisers, Buddha focused on the feelings of the conquered (hatred), and contentment as the key to happiness, not outward circumstances.

Day 169

Solomon

Hatred stirs up strife, but love covers all transgressions.[335]

Better a meal of vegetables where there is love than a fattened calf with hatred.[336]

Buddha

[202] There is no fire like passion; there is no losing throw like hatred; there is no pain like this body; there is no happiness higher than rest.

Hatred is a losing proposition. It stirs up bitter conflict and discord. Love is the antidote. Better to have a bowl of vegetables with love and contentment, than to have the finest feast with hate in our hearts.

---

[333] Proverbs 2:7 (NIV).
[334] Proverbs 11:14 (NIV).
[335] Proverbs 10:12 (NASB).
[336] Proverbs 15:17 (NIV).

Day 170

Solomon

Buddha

Men do not despise a thief if he steals to satisfy his hunger when he is starving.[337]

The laborer's appetite works for him; his hunger drives him on.[338]

[203] Hunger is the worst of diseases, the body the greatest of pains; if one knows this truly, that is Nirvana, the highest happiness.

    Hunger is a powerful, painful force in our lives. How we fulfill that ongoing need can be righteous and blessed or wicked and destructive.

---

[337] Proverbs 6:30 (NIV).
[338] Proverbs 16:26 (NIV).

Day 171

Solomon

Buddha

Be not wise in your own eyes; reverently fear and worship the Lord and turn [entirely] away from evil. It shall be health to your nerves and sinews, and marrow and moistening to your bones.[339]

[204] Health is the greatest of gifts, contentedness the best riches; trust is the best of relationships, Nirvana the highest happiness.

Do not let them [wisdom and understanding] depart from your sight; keep them in the midst of your heart. For they are life to those who find them and health to all their body.[340]

Good health is a great gift. Turning completely away from evil and keeping wisdom paramount in our lives, breathes life and health into us.

---

[339] Proverbs 3:7-8 (AMP).
[340] Proverbs 4:21-22 (NASB).

Day 172

Solomon

Two are better than one, because they have a good return for their work: if one falls down, his friend can help him up. But pity the man who falls and has no one to help him up! Also, if two lie down together, they will keep warm. But how can one keep warm alone? Though one may be overpowered, two can defend themselves. A cord of three strands is not quickly broken.[341]

Buddha

[205] He who has tasted the sweetness of solitude and tranquillity [sic], is free from fear and free from sin, while he tastes the sweetness of drinking in the law.

There are virtues to be found in companionship and solitude. Solomon wrote about how with a companion, there is an increase in their productivity, they are able to help when one falls, and they are better equipped to defend themselves against an aggressor. Buddha taught about the sweetness of solitude and the ability to meditate on the law without interruption.

---

[341] Ecclesiastes 4:9-12 (NIV).

Day 173

Solomon

He who walks with wise men will be wise, but the companion of fools will suffer harm.[342]

Go from the presence of a foolish man, when you do not perceive in him the lips of knowledge.[343]

Buddha

[206] The sight of the elect (Arya) is good, to live with them is always happiness; if a man does not see fools, he will be truly happy.

Our choices in friendship and companionship are important. Time spent with a wise person assists us in growing wiser. Time spent with a fool can bring us harm.

---

[342] Proverbs 13:20 (NASB).
[343] Proverbs 14:7 (NKJV).

Day 174

Solomon	Buddha
Do not speak to a fool, for he will scorn the wisdom of your words.[344]	[207] He who walks in the company of fools suffers a long way; company with fools, as with an enemy, is always painful; company with the wise is pleasure, like meeting with kinsfolk.
It is better to listen to the rebuke of a wise man than for one to listen to the song of fools.[345]	

Better to spend time with a wise man, and even suffer his rebuke, than to be a companion of a fool, even a fool who perhaps has talent, such as one who is a proficient singer or musician, and suffer for it.

---

[344] Proverbs 23:9 (NIV).
[345] Ecclesiastes 7:5 (NASB).

Day 175

Solomon	Buddha
Walk with the wise and become wise. . . .[346]	[208] Therefore, one ought to follow the wise, the intelligent, the learned, the much enduring, the dutiful, the elect; one ought to follow a good and wise man, as the moon follows the path of the stars.

Walk with the wise. Learn from the intelligent, learned and dutiful. Follow after them as naturally as the moon follows the stars. As we make this a habit in our lives, we will see the positive consequences of it.

---

[346] Proverbs 13:20a (NIV).

Chapter Sixteen – Pleasure

(Days 176-187, Dhammapada 209-220)

This chapter discusses the pitfalls of pleasure. Vanity, envy, pain, grief and fear can drive us to seek pleasure. The unabashed pursuit of pleasure can turn around and result in more grief, fear, poverty and heartache.

Living in moderation, without extremes, is a valuable course.

Affection and lust can result in grief, and lust acted upon can bring dire consequences into our lives.

When wisdom is more precious to us than material wealth and pleasure, we know a peace that is beyond words, and we are free from chains of evil deeds and pleasure.

Day 176

Solomon (950 BCE)

Before destruction the heart of a man is haughty, and before honor is humility.[347]

A calm and undisturbed mind and heart are the life and health of the body, but envy, jealousy, and wrath are like rottenness of the bones.[348]

Buddha (525 BCE)

[209] He who gives himself to vanity, and does not give himself to meditation, forgetting the real aim (of life) and grasping at pleasure, will in time envy him who has exerted himself in meditation.

The one who gives himself over to vanity and is haughty, is heading for a fall, and when he falls, he will envy the one who is calm and tranquil and has spent time meditating. Envy will then compound his fall, rotting his very bones.

---

[347] Proverbs 18:12 (NKJV).
[348] Proverbs 14:30 (AMP).

Day 177

Solomon

For wisdom will enter your heart and knowledge will be pleasant to your soul.[349]

Blessed is the man who finds wisdom, the man who gains understanding, for she is more profitable than silver and yields better returns than gold. She is more precious than rubies; nothing you desire can compare with her.[350]

Buddha

[210] Let no man ever look for what is pleasant, or what is unpleasant. Not to see what is pleasant is pain, and it is pain to see what is unpleasant.

We ought not to put the cart before the horse. Finding what is pleasant or pleasurable is not the primary pursuit. Pursuing wisdom, knowledge, and understanding is paramount.

---

[349] Proverbs 2:10 (NASB).
[350] Proverbs 3:13-15 (NIV).

Day 178

Solomon

Buddha

Let love and faithfulness never leave you; bind them around your neck, write them on the tablet of your heart.[351]

A friend loves at all times. . .[352]

He who pursues righteousness and love finds life, prosperity and honor.[353]

[211] Let, therefore, no man love anything; loss of the beloved is evil. Those who love nothing and hate nothing, have no fetters.

Solomon advocated loving at all times. Buddha advocated having neither love nor hate, as both lead to being fettered to another, and the loss of a loved one is painful.

---

[351] Proverbs 3:3 (NIV).
[352] Proverbs 17:17a (NASB).
[353] Proverbs 21:21 (NIV).

Day 179

Solomon

Buddha

Even in laughter the heart may be in pain, and the end of joy may be grief.[354]

He who loves pleasure will become poor; whoever loves wine and oil will never be rich.[355]

[212] From pleasure comes grief, from pleasure comes fear; he who is free from pleasure knows neither grief nor fear.

The unabashed pursuit of pleasure can result in grief, fear, poverty, and heartache. Living in moderation, without extremes, is a valuable course.

---

[354] Proverbs 14:13 (NASB).
[355] Proverbs 21:17 (NIV).

Day 180

Solomon	Buddha
Let not mercy and kindness [shutting out all hatred and selfishness] and truth [shutting out all deliberate hypocrisy or falsehood] forsake you; bind them about your neck, write them upon the tablet of your heart. So shall you find favor, good understanding, and high esteem in the sight [or judgment] of God and man.[356]	[213] From affection comes grief, from affection comes fear; he who is free from affection knows neither grief nor fear.

He who pursues righteousness and love finds life, prosperity and honor.[357]

Affection, as in an unhealthy attachment, can result in grief and fear, but Solomon advocates pursuing righteousness, faithfulness and love. He wrote that it results in a good reputation and prosperity, winning the favor of God and man.

---

[356] Proverbs 3:3-4 (AMP).
[357] Proverbs 21:21 (NIV).

Day 181

Solomon

Lust not after her beauty in your heart, neither let her capture you with her eyelids. For on account of a harlot a man is brought to a piece of bread, and the adulteress stalks and snares [as with a hook] the precious life [of a man]. Can a man take fire in his bosom and his clothes not be burned? Can one go upon hot coals and his feet not be burned? So he who cohabits with his neighbor's wife [will be tortured with evil consequences and just retribution]; he who touches her shall not be innocent or go unpunished.[358]

Buddha

[214] From lust comes grief, from lust comes fear; he who is free from lust knows neither grief nor fear.

Lust, acted upon, can bring dire consequences: the ruin of a man, his reputation, and his family. When we seek after a prostitute, or an adulterous relationship, it is like we are taking a torch to our lives. Jesus went so far as to teach, "But I tell you that anyone who looks at a woman lustfully has already committed adultery with her in his heart."[359]

---

[358] Proverbs 6:25-29 (AMP).
[359] Matthew 5:28 (NIV).

Day 182

Solomon

Let not mercy and truth forsake you; bind them around your neck, write them on the tablet of your heart, and so find favor and high esteem in the sight of God and man.[360]

Better is a dinner of herbs where love is, than a fatted calf with hatred.[361]

A friend loves at all times, and a brother is born for adversity.[362]

Buddha

[215] From love comes grief, from love comes fear; he who is free from love knows neither grief nor fear.

Solomon taught that when we have unselfish, unconditional love for those around us, it blesses them. Buddha taught that love as a selfish attachment brings grief and fear. It will be a burden not easily set aside.

---

[360] Proverbs 3:3-4 (NKJV).
[361] Proverbs 15:17 (NKJV).
[362] Proverbs 17:17 (NASB).

Day 183

Solomon

He who is greedy for gain troubles his own house, but he who hates bribes will live.[363]

He who is of a greedy spirit stirs up strife, but he who puts his trust in the Lord shall be enriched and blessed.[364]

Better the little that the righteous have than the wealth of many wicked.[365]

Buddha

[216] From greed comes grief, from greed comes fear; he who is free from greed knows neither grief nor fear.

When we are greedy, it brings trouble upon us. From greed comes grief, fear and dissension. We are better off to have little with peace and righteousness than great wealth with great trouble.

---

[363] Proverbs 15:27 (NKJV).
[364] Proverbs 28:25 (AMP).
[365] Psalm 37:16 (NIV), a psalm of King David, Solomon's father.

Day 184

Solomon

Where there is no revelation, the people cast off restraint; but happy is he who keeps the law.[366]

To do righteousness and justice is desired by the Lord more than sacrifice.[367]

Buddha

[217] He who possesses virtue and intelligence, who is just, speaks the truth, and does what is his own business, him the world will hold dear.

If we possess virtue (righteousness) and intelligence (understanding), are just, speak the truth, and mind our own business, we will be blessed. King David taught:

> Lord, who may dwell in your sanctuary? Who may live on your holy hill? He whose walk is blameless and who does what is righteous, who speaks the truth from his heart and has no slander on his tongue, who does his neighbor no wrong and casts no slur on his fellowman, who despises a vile man but honors those who fear the Lord, who keeps his oath even when it hurts, who lends his money without usury and does not accept a bribe against the innocent. He who does these things will never be shaken.[368]

---

[366] Proverbs 29:18 (NKJV).
[367] Proverbs 21:3 (NASB).
[368] Psalm 15:1-5 (NIV), a psalm of King David, Solomon's father.

Day 185

Solomon	Buddha

For wisdom is more precious than rubies, and nothing you desire can compare with her.[369]

My son, keep my words and treasure my commandments within you. Keep my commandments and live, and my teaching as the apple of your eye. Bind them on your fingers; write them on the tablet of your heart.[370]

[218] He in whom a desire for the Ineffable (Nirvana) has sprung up, who is satisfied in his mind, and whose thoughts are not bewildered by love, he is called urdhvamsrotas (carried upwards by the stream).

When wisdom is more precious to us than material wealth, and we treasure and keep the law in our hearts and mind, we know a peace that is beyond words, and we are free from the chains of sin.

---

[369] Proverbs 8:11 (NIV).
[370] Proverbs 7:1–3 (NASB).

Day 186

Solomon	Buddha

Solomon

A friend loves at all times, and a brother is born for adversity.[371]

If one falls down, his friend can help him up. But pity the man who falls and has no one to help him up![372]

Buddha

[219] Kinsmen, friends, and lovers salute a man who has been long away, and returns safe from afar.

What is sweeter than to be greeted with love and affection by our friends and family after a safe return home from a long journey, and what a joy to be lifted up when we have fallen by a dear friend. Let us remember to be good and loving to our friends and family.

---

[371] Proverbs 17:17 (NKJV).
[372] Ecclesiastes 4:10 (NIV).

Day 187

Solomon	Buddha

But he [the simple] knows not that the shades of the dead are there [specters haunting the scene of past transgressions], and that her invited guests are [already sunk] in the depths of Sheol (the lower world, Hades, the place of the dead).[373]

[220] In like manner his good works receive him who has done good, and has gone from this world to the other;—as kinsmen receive a friend on his return.

When calamity comes, the wicked are brought down, but even in death the righteous seek refuge in God.[374]

Solomon taught that the simple can be led astray by keeping unruly company, under the spectre of those who already dwell in Sheol or Hades. He also said that in death the righteous seek refuge in God, implying that a life with God is possible after death. The Buddha's teaching carries the underlying assumption of karma. He taught that a person's good works will receive them after death like a friend or brother receives one after a long journey.

---

[373] Proverbs 9:18 (AMP).
[374] Proverbs 14:32 (NIV).

Chapter Seventeen – Anger

(Days 188-200, Dhammapada 221-234)

Chapter Seventeen expounds on the consequences of anger. Anger can cause us to act rashly, stir up an entire city and drive away friends and family. Love subdues and dissipates anger.

We cannot expect to always be liked or praised. Let us not be swayed by other people's opinion of us, whether good or bad.

Anger can blind us from seeing what's really important.

Self-control is essential to leading a righteous life. The wise control their mind, tongue and body, for without self-control, we are ruined.

Day 188

Solomon (950 BCE)

Scoffers set a city afire [inflaming the minds of the people], but wise men turn away wrath.[375]

A gentle answer turns away wrath, but a harsh word stirs up anger.[376]

Do not make friends with a hot-tempered man, do not associate with one easily angered.[377]

Buddha (525 BCE)

[221] Let a man leave anger, let him forsake pride, let him overcome all bondage! No sufferings befall the man who is not attached to name and form, and who calls nothing his own.

Anger drives a man like a car raging out of control, only disaster awaits. It can stir up an entire city and drive away friends. We are better off to exert self-control, not be quickly provoked, and reply gently, which can diffuse anger.

---

[375] Proverbs 29:8 (AMP).
[376] Proverbs 15:1 (NASB).
[377] Proverbs 22:24 (NIV).

Day 189

Solomon

Buddha

A fool gives full vent to his anger, but a wise man keeps himself under control.[378]

Do not be eager in your heart to be angry, for anger resides in the bosom of fools.[379]

[222] He who holds back rising anger like a rolling chariot, him I call a real driver; other people are but holding the reins.

Fools rant and rage, out of control with anger. We ought to hang onto the reins of our emotions and not let anger drive us.

---

[378] Proverbs 29:11 (NIV).
[379] Ecclesiastes 7:9 (NASB).

Day 190

Solomon

Buddha

Through love and faithfulness sin is atoned for . . .[380]

The wicked borrow and do not repay, but the righteous give generously.[381]

Good will come to him who is generous and lends freely, who conducts his affairs with justice.[382]

Do they not go astray who devise evil? But mercy and truth belong to those who devise good.[383]

Keep falsehood and lies far from me; give me neither poverty nor riches, but give me only my daily bread.[384]

[223] Let a man overcome anger by love, let him overcome evil by good; let him overcome the greedy by liberality, the liar by truth!

Love subdues and dissipates anger, good vanquishes evil, generosity overcomes greed, and the truth outshines the darkness of lies. Let us pursue doing good, being loving and generous, and speaking the truth.

---

[380] Proverbs 16:6a (NIV).
[381] Psalm 37:21 (NIV), a psalm of King David, Solomon's father.
[382] Psalm 112:5 (NIV).
[383] Proverbs 14:22 (NKJV).
[384] Proverbs 30:8 (NIV). Proverbs 30 is attributed to Agur, son of Jakeh.

Day 191

Solomon

Buddha

Kings take pleasure in honest lips; they value a man who speaks the truth.[385]

A [self-confident] fool utters all his anger, but a wise man holds it back and stills it.[386]

He who gives to the poor will lack nothing, but he who closes his eyes to them receives many curses.[387]

[224] Speak the truth, do not yield to anger; give, if thou art asked for little; by these three steps thou wilt go near the gods.

Speak truthfully, do not give in to anger, and be generous. These three steps lift our lives to a new level of understanding and righteousness. In Psalms we read, "Good will come to him who is generous and lends freely, who conducts his affairs with justice."[388]

---

[385] Proverbs 16:13 (NIV).
[386] Proverbs 29:11 (AMP).
[387] Proverbs 28:27 (NIV).
[388] Psalm 112:5 (NIV).

Day 192

Solomon	Buddha
The one whose walk is blameless is kept safe, but the one whose ways are perverse will fall into the pit.[389]	[225] The sages who injure nobody, and who always control their body, they will go to the unchangeable place (Nirvana), where, if they have gone, they will suffer no more.
He who is slow to anger is better than the mighty, and he who rules his spirit than he who takes a city.[390]	

Self-control is essential to living a righteous life, for without it, our lives become chaotic and destructive. King David taught, "Be not like the horse or the mule, which lack understanding, which must have their mouths held firm with bit and bridle, or else they will not come with you."[391]

---

[389] Proverbs 28:18 (NIV).
[390] Proverbs 16:32 (NKJV).
[391] Psalm 32:9 (AMP), a psalm of King David, Solomon's father.

Day 193

Solomon	Buddha

Oh, how I love your law! I meditate on it all day long.[392]

At midnight I will rise to give thanks to You because of Your righteous ordinances.[393]

[226] Those who are ever watchful, who study day and night, and who strive after Nirvana, their passions will come to an end.

Those who meditate on and delight in the law day and night are blessed.

Blessed is the man who does not walk in the counsel of the wicked or stand in the way of sinners or sit in the seat of mockers. But his delight is in the law of the LORD, and on his law he meditates day and night. He is like a tree planted by streams of water, which yields its fruit in season and whose leaf does not wither. Whatever he does prospers.[394]

---

[392] Psalm 119:97 (NIV).
[393] Psalm 119:62 (AMP).
[394] Psalm 1:1-3 (NIV), a psalm of King David, Solomon's father.

Day 194

Solomon

Buddha

The bloodthirsty hate the blameless man, but the upright care for and seek [to save] his life.[395]

Indeed, there is not a righteous man on earth who continually does good and who never sins.[396]

[227] This is an old saying, O Atula, this is not only of to-day: 'They blame him who sits silent, they blame him who speaks much, they also blame him who says little; there is no one on earth who is not blamed.'

It's impossible to please everyone. There will always be someone who will say this person speaks too much or too little, does too much or too little, but we can make the effort to live a righteous life and not to do harm.

---

[395] Proverbs 29:10 (AMP).
[396] Ecclesiastes 7:20 (NASB).

Day 195

Solomon

Buddha

A man will be praised according to his insight, but one of perverse mind will be despised.[397]

Let another praise you, and not your own mouth; someone else, and not your own lips.[398]

[228] There never was, there never will be, nor is there now, a man who is always blamed, or a man who is always praised.

Being praised and being blamed can be problematic. We might find ourselves changing because of other people's opinions. If praised, we might become self-deprecating to a fault, or being blamed, we might begin praising ourselves. As much is as possible, let us not be swayed by opinion, unless it is a valid admonishment.

---

[397] Proverbs 12:8 (NASB).
[398] Proverbs 27:2 (NIV).

Day 196

Solomon

The crucible for silver and the furnace for gold, but man is tested by the praise he receives.[399]

Buddha

[229, 230.] But he whom those who discriminate praise continually day after day, as without blemish, wise, rich in knowledge and virtue, who would dare to blame him, like a coin made of gold from the Gambu river? Even the gods praise him, he is praised even by Brahman.

If we are wise, being praised can refine us. It tests our knowledge and virtue. If we harbor pride, it can feed the pride until it's out of control, but if we are humble and discriminating, we will not be swayed by praise or blame.

---

[399] Proverbs 27:21 (NIV).

Day 197

Solomon

Buddha

A fool always loses his temper, but a wise man holds it back.[400]

Do not be quickly provoked in your spirit, for anger resides in the lap of fools.[401]

[231] Beware of bodily anger, and control thy body! Leave the sins of the body, and with thy body practise [sic] virtue!

Anger is destructive on many levels. It can prompt us to act rashly and cause harm to other. It can drive people away from us and destroy our relationships. It can cause us bodily harm (i.e., facilitate the development of disease). It can blind us from seeing what's really important in a situation, and keep us from doing more important things that need our attention. King David taught, "In your anger do not sin; when you are on your beds, search your hearts and be silent."[402] And, "Cease from anger, and forsake wrath; do not fret—it only causes harm."[403]

[400] Proverbs 29:11 (NASB).
[401] Ecclesiastes 7:9 (NIV).
[402] Psalm 4:4 (NIV), a psalm of King David, Solomon's father.
[403] Psalm 37:8 (NKJV), a psalm of King David, Solomon's father.

Day 198

Solomon

Buddha

Put away from you a deceitful mouth and put devious speech far from you.[404]

[232] Beware of the anger of the tongue, and control thy tongue! Leave the sins of the tongue, and practise [*sic*] virtue with thy tongue!

The tongue can be a destructive force. We do well to guard it. With our words, we can speak the truth or be deceitful, we can speak faithfully or betray trust, we can speak with love and kindness or with hate and anger. Every time we speak, we have a choice. Let us choose wisely.

---

[404] Proverbs 4:24 (NASB).

Day 199

Solomon

He who is slow to anger is better than the mighty, and he who rules his spirit than he who takes a city.[405]

Above all else, guard your heart, for it is the wellspring of life.[406]

A man is praised according to his wisdom, but men with warped minds are despised.[407]

Buddha

[233] Beware of the anger of the mind, and control thy mind! Leave the sins of the mind, and practise [sic] virtue with thy mind!

Guarding our hearts and minds from evil and having control over our emotions and our thinking are vitally important parts of living a righteous life. James, the brother of Jesus, wrote to the twelve scattered tribes of Israel,

> So then, my beloved brethren, let every man be swift to hear, slow to speak, slow to wrath; for the wrath of man does not produce the righteousness of God.[408]

---

[405] Proverbs 16:32 (NKJV).
[406] Proverbs 4:23 (NIV).
[407] Proverbs 12:8 (NIV).
[408] James 1:19-20 (NKJV).

Day 200

Solomon

Buddha

Like a city whose walls are broken down is a man who lacks self-control.[409]

[234] The wise who control their body, who control their tongue, the wise who control their mind, are indeed well controlled.

The wise control their body, mind and tongue. Without self-control, our lives become like a decaying city without any protective walls.

---

[409] Proverbs 25:28 (NIV).

Chapter Eighteen – Impurity

(Days 201-220, Dhammapada 235-255)

This chapter focuses on removing impurities from our lives. Minding our own business, studying to be wise, working hard, doing good, and filling our minds with knowledge and wisdom drive away impurities.

It is important to avoid sloth and thoughtlessness in prayer, work and our personal lives. Living with a pure heart takes effort, like tending a garden. We need to be diligent to remove the weeds of selfishness that would choke out purity in our hearts.

Day 201

Solomon (950 BCE)

Wisdom will save you from the ways of wicked men, from men whose words are perverse, who leave the straight paths to walk in dark ways, who delight in doing wrong and rejoice in the perverseness of evil, whose paths are crooked and who are devious in their ways.[410]

There is a way that seems right to a man, but in the end it leads to death.[411]

Buddha (525 BCE)

[235] Thou art now like a sear leaf, the messengers of death (Yama) have come near to thee; thou standest [*sic*] at the door of thy departure, and thou hast no provision for thy journey.

Without wisdom, we might think wrong is right and evil is good. We wouldn't know which way to turn. We cannot journey through this life without wisdom to equip us when evil approaches us.

---

[410] Proverbs 2:11-15 (NIV).
[411] Proverbs 14:12 (NIV).

Day 202

Solomon	**Buddha**

Whatever your hand finds to do, do it with all your might. . . .[412]

From the fruit of his words a man shall be satisfied with good, and the work of a man's hands shall come back to him [as a harvest].[413]

[236] Make thyself an island, work hard, be wise! When thy impurities are blown away, and thou art free from guilt, thou wilt enter into the heavenly world of the elect (Ariya).

To mind our own business, study to be wise, and work hard is a recipe for purifying us from evil. The Apostle Paul wrote to the Thessalonians, "Make it your ambition to lead a quiet life, to mind your own business and to work with your hands, just as we told you."[414]

---

[412] Ecclesiastes 9:10a (NIV).
[413] Proverbs 12:14 (AMP).
[414] 1 Thessalonians 4:11 (NIV).

Day 203

Solomon

Buddha

Better to go to the house of mourning than to go to the house of feasting, for that is the end of all men; and the living will take it to heart.[415]

[237] Thy life has come to an end, thou art come near to death (Yama), there is no resting-place for thee on the road, and thou hast no provision for thy journey.

All men die. This we cannot escape. How much better to spend this life in goodness and righteousness. In Psalms we read, about the inevitability of death,

> You turn men back to dust, saying, "Return to dust, O sons of men." For a thousand years in your sight are like a day that has just gone by, or like a watch in the night. You sweep men away in the sleep of death; they are like the new grass of the morning—though in the morning it springs up new, by evening it is dry and withered.[416]

---

[415] Ecclesiastes 7:2 (NKJV).
[416] Psalm 90:3-6 (NIV).

Day 204

Solomon	Buddha
All hard work brings a profit, but mere talk leads only to poverty.[417]	[238] Make thyself an island, work hard, be wise! When thy impurities are blown away, and thou art free from guilt, thou wilt not enter again into birth and decay.

As in Dhammapada 236, in 238 Buddha repeats the importance of minding our own business, working hard, and studying to be wise.

Day 205

Solomon	Buddha
Remove the dross from the silver, and out comes material for the silversmith.[418]	[239] Let a wise man blow off the impurities of his self, as a smith blows off the impurities of silver one by one, little by little, and from time to time.

As we study to be wise, and implement wise behavior into our lives, we skim away the "dross" and purify ourselves.

---

[417] Proverbs 14:23 (NIV).
[418] Proverbs 25:4 (NIV).

Day 206

Solomon

Buddha

For the waywardness of the simple will kill them, and the complacency of fools will destroy them.[419]

. . . fools die for lack of judgment.[420]

[240] As the impurity which springs from the iron, when it springs from it, destroys it; thus do a transgressor's own works lead him to the evil path.

Impurities come from within. That is why we need to pursue wisdom and righteousness. Otherwise, it is our evil deeds and foolishness that will be our undoing. Jesus taught,

> But those things which proceed out of the mouth come from the heart, and they defile a man. For out of the heart proceed evil thoughts, murders, adulteries, fornications, thefts, false witness, blasphemies. These are the things which defile a man, but to eat with unwashed hands does not defile a man.[421]

---

[419] Proverbs 1:32 (NIV).
[420] Proverbs 10:21b (NIV).
[421] Matthew 15:18–20 (NKJV).

Day 207

Solomon

Buddha

Through indolence the rafters sag, and through slackness the house leaks.[422]

The way of the sluggard is overgrown with thorns [it pricks, lacerates, and entangles him], but the way of the righteous is plain and raised like a highway.[423]

[241] The taint of prayers is non-repetition; the taint of houses, non- repair; the taint of the body is sloth; the taint of a watchman, thought-lessness.

Sloth and thoughtlessness in prayer, work, and maintenance of our dwellings and bodies taints our life. Let us be watchful, diligent, and eager to learn and work hard. Let us actively take care of our responsibilities in life.

---

[422] Ecclesiastes 10:18 (NASB).
[423] Proverbs 15:19 (AMP).

Day 208

Solomon

And I discovered more bitter than death the woman whose heart is snares and nets, whose hands are chains. One who is pleasing to God will escape from her, but the sinner will be captured by her.[424]

As a ring of gold in a swine's snout, so is a lovely woman who lacks discretion.[425]

A greedy man brings trouble to his family, but he who hates bribes will live.[426]

Buddha

[242] Bad conduct is the taint of woman, greediness the taint of a benefactor; tainted are all evil ways in this world and in the next.

A woman without discretion, who is seriously looking to trap a man, and a greedy man or woman, will bring harm and trouble to others and themselves.

---

[424] Ecclesiastes 7:26 (NASB).
[425] Proverbs 11:22 (NKJV).
[426] Proverbs 15:27 (NIV).

Day 209

Solomon

Get wisdom! Get understanding! Do not forget, nor turn away from the words of my mouth. Do not forsake her, and she will preserve you; Love her, and she will keep you. Wisdom is the principal thing; Therefore get wisdom. And in all your getting, get understanding.[427]

Buddha

[243] But there is a taint worse than all taints,—ignorance is the greatest taint. O mendicants! throw off that taint, and become taintless!

The cure for ignorance is getting wisdom and understanding. We ought to seek them out diligently, daily, and with great perseverance.

---

[427] Proverbs 4:5–7 (NKJV).

Day 210

Solomon

Before his downfall a man's heart is proud, but humility comes before honor. He who answers before listening— that is his folly and his shame.[428]

The curse of the LORD is on the house of the wicked, but He blesses the home of the just. Surely He scorns the scornful, but gives grace to the humble. The wise shall inherit glory, but shame shall be the legacy of fools.[429]

Buddha

[244] Life is easy to live for a man who is without shame, a crow hero, a mischief-maker, an insulting, bold, and wretched fellow.

Living in pride and recklessness is a foolish way to go. It may seem easy in the beginning to live selfishly, without concern for others, but before long it will bring shame and a downfall.

---

[428] Proverbs 18:12-13 (NIV).
[429] Proverbs 3:33-35 (NKJV).

Day 211

Solomon

I went past the field of the sluggard, past the vineyard of the man who lacks judgment; thorns had come up everywhere, the ground was covered with weeds, and the stone wall was in ruins.[430]

The LORD detests the thoughts of the wicked, but those of the pure are pleasing to him.[431]

Buddha

[245] But life is hard to live for a modest man, who always looks for what is pure, who is disinterested, quiet, spotless, and intelligent.

Living with a pure heart takes effort. Like tending a garden, we need to be diligent to remove the weeds of selfishness that would choke out purity in our hearts.

---

[430] Proverbs 24:30-31 (NIV).
[431] Proverbs 15:26 (NIV).

Day 212

Solomon

Part of the Ten Commandments:

- You shall not murder.
- You shall not commit adultery.
- You shall not steal.
- You shall not give false testimony against your neighbor.
- You shall not covet your neighbor's house. You shall not covet your neighbor's wife, or his manservant or maidservant, his ox or donkey, or anything that belongs to your neighbor.[432]

Buddha

[246] He who destroys life, who speaks untruth, who in this world takes what is not given him, who goes to another man's wife;

Wealth gained by dishonesty will be diminished, but he who gathers by labor will increase.[433]

Bread obtained by falsehood is sweet to a man, but afterward his mouth will be filled with gravel.[434]

Mankind always needs to be reminded that killing, lying, stealing, and committing adultery are wrong. We ought not to live that way. It harms others and ourselves.

---

[432] Exodus 20:13–17 (NIV). Moses lived at least 200 years prior to Solomon.
[433] Proverbs 13:11 (NKJV).
[434] Proverbs 20:17 (NASB).

Day 213

Solomon	Buddha

Listen, my son, and be wise, and keep your heart on the right path. Do not join those who drink too much wine or gorge themselves on meat, for drunkards and gluttons become poor, and drowsiness clothes them in rags.[435]

[247] And the man who gives himself to drinking intoxicating liquors, he, even in this world, digs up his own root.

Drinking too much and associating with others who drink too much are destructive forces in our lives. Moderation is sensible and valuable to leading a mindful, righteous life.

---

[435] Proverbs 23:19-21 (NIV).

Day 214

Solomon	**Buddha**
Whoever has no rule over his own spirit is like a city broken down, without walls.[436] He who is greedy for unjust gain troubles his own household, but he who hates bribes will live.[437]	[248] O man, know this, that the unrestrained are in a bad state; take care that greediness and vice do not bring thee to grief for a long time!

A lack of self-control and greediness is a bad combination. It will bring down trouble and grief upon us and our household. Let us be content with a moderate, self-restrained life.

---

[436] Proverbs 25:28 (NKJV).
[437] Proverbs 15:27 (AMP).

Day 215

Solomon

The righteous is concerned for the rights of the poor, the wicked does not understand such concern.[438]

Buddha

[249] The world gives according to their faith or according to their pleasure: if a man frets about the food and the drink given to others, he will find no rest either by day or by night.

Let our charitable deeds be done with a generous heart and not for any self-serving reasons, such as desiring the notice or praise of others. Let us not worry about what we have given to others. Let us live in contentment. Jesus taught,

> *Take heed that you do not do your charitable deeds before men, to be seen by them. Otherwise you have no reward from your Father in heaven. Therefore, when you do a charitable deed, do not sound a trumpet before you as the hypocrites do in the synagogues and in the streets, that they may have glory from men. Assuredly, I say to you, they have their reward. But when you do a charitable deed, do not let your left hand know what your right hand is doing, that your charitable deed may be in secret; and your Father who sees in secret will Himself reward you openly.[439]*

---

[438] Proverbs 29:7 (NASB).
[439] Matthew 6:1–4 (NKJV).

Day 216

Solomon

Buddha

A generous man will himself be blessed, for he shares his food with the poor.[440]

A generous man will prosper; he who refreshes others will himself be refreshed.[441]

[250] He in whom that feeling [of the worry of what he has given to others] is destroyed, and taken out with the very root, finds rest by day and by night.

In the fifth book of Moses, it is written,

> You shall generously give to him [the poor], and your heart shall not be grieved when you give to him, because for this thing the LORD your God will bless you in all your work and in all your undertakings.[442]

Rather than worrying about what we have given to others, if we give generously, we will be refreshed, blessed and free from worry.

---

[440] Proverbs 22:9 (NIV).
[441] Proverbs 11:25 (NIV).
[442] Deuteronomy 15:10 (NASB). Moses lived at least 200 years prior to Solomon.

Day 217

Solomon

He who trusts in his riches will fall, but the righteous will flourish like the green leaf.[443]

Better is a little with righteousness, than vast revenues without justice.[444]

Wealth is worthless in the day of wrath, but righteousness delivers from death.[445]

Buddha

[251] There is no fire like passion, there is no shark like hatred, there is no snare like folly, there is no torrent like greed.

The Apostle Paul wrote,

> People who want to get rich fall into temptation and a trap and into many foolish and harmful desires that plunge men into ruin and destruction. For the love of money is a root of all kinds of evil. Some people, eager for money, have wandered from the faith and pierced themselves with many griefs.[446]

If we trust in money and allow greed to grow in our hearts and minds, we are liable to forget all about living a righteous life. When troubles come, all the money in the world cannot come to our aid. Better to have a little with wisdom and righteousness, than a fat bank account and foolishness.

---

[443] Proverbs 11:28 (NASB).
[444] Proverbs 16:8 (NKJV).
[445] Proverbs 11:4 (NIV).
[446] 1 Timothy 6:9-10 (NIV).

Day 218

Solomon	**Buddha**

Fools mock at making amends for sin, but goodwill is found among the upright.[447]

252 The fault of others is easily perceived, but that of oneself is difficult to perceive; a man winnows his neighbour's [sic] faults like chaff, but his own fault he hides, as a cheat hides the bad die from the gambler.

Better to take care of correcting our own faults, rather than spend time looking for the faults of others. Better to carefully winnow out the evil in our own life, and have goodwill towards others than to find ourselves judging others while allowing evil to grow in our lives. Jesus taught,

> Judge not, that you be not judged. For with what judgment you judge, you will be judged; and with the measure you use, it will be measured back to you. And why do you look at the speck in your brother's eye, but do not consider the plank in your own eye? Or how can you say to your brother, "Let me remove the speck from your eye"; and look, a plank is in your own eye? Hypocrite! First remove the plank from your own eye, and then you will see clearly to remove the speck from your brother's eye.[448]

---

[447] Proverbs 14:9 (NIV).
[448] Matthew 7:1–5 (NKJV).

Day 219

Solomon

Buddha

Will they not go astray who devise evil? But kindness and truth will be to those who devise good.[449]

[253] If a man looks after the faults of others, and is always inclined to be offended, his own passions will grow, and he is far from the destruction of passions.

If we have kindness and goodwill toward others, there is no room for judging or faultfinding. If we spend our time judging others, we might allow evil to grow in our own lives.

---

[449] Proverbs 14:22 (NASB).

Day 220

Solomon

The LORD's curse is on the house of the wicked, but he blesses the home of the righteous. He mocks proud mockers but gives grace to the humble. The wise inherit honor, but fools he holds up to shame.[450]

Before destruction the heart of man is haughty, and before honour [sic] is humility.[451]

Buddha

[254] There is no path through the air, a man is not a Samana by outward acts. The world delights in vanity, the Tathagatas (the Buddhas) are free from vanity.

[255] There is no path through the air, a man is not a Samana by outward acts. No creatures are eternal; but the awakened (Buddha) are never shaken.

The importance of being free from excessive pride in one's abilities, achievements and appearance, and from being arrogant or disdainfully proud, is a key element to the righteous life. Let us strive to be free from being vain, proud and haughty, and to have a humble spirit, so that we will not be shaken from our path.

[450] Proverbs 3:33-35 (NIV).
[451] Proverbs 18:12 (KJV).

Chapter Nineteen – The Just

(Days 221-233, Dhammapada 256-272)

This chapter discusses attributes of the just, such as being able to discern right from wrong, being attentive to studying the law, being full of wisdom and knowledge, having seasoned and restrained speech, and having a life filled with truth, virtue, love and moderation.

Envy, greed and anger (violence) are contrary to being a person of integrity, who is whole and honest with a sound moral character.

Having kindness and pity toward all people and animals is a distinguishing trait of the righteous and just.

Day 221

Solomon (950 BCE)

My son, if you accept my words and store up my commands within you, turning your ear to wisdom and applying your heart to understanding, and if you call out for insight and cry aloud for understanding, and if you look for it as for silver and search for it as for hidden treasure, then you will understand the fear of the LORD and find the knowledge of God.

Then you will understand what is right and just and fair—every good path. For wisdom will enter your heart, and knowledge will be pleasant to your soul. Discretion will protect you, and understanding will guard you.[452]

Buddha (525 BCE)

[256, 257.] A man is not just if he carries a matter by violence; no, he who distinguishes both right and wrong, who is learned and leads others, not by violence, but by law and equity, and who is guarded by the law and intelligent, he is called just.

Being able to distinguish between right and wrong, being learned, full of wisdom and knowledge, being a leader not through violence, but leading through the knowledge of what is right and fair, and being guarded by the law, wisdom, knowledge and discretion, by all these traits a person is known to be just. Let us strive to be that type of person.

---

[452] Proverbs 2:1-5, 9-11 (NIV).

Day 222

Solomon

Buddha

In a multitude of words transgression is not lacking, but he who restrains his lips is prudent.[453]

A fool vents all his feelings, but a wise man holds them back.[454]

Idle chatter leads only to poverty.[455]

[258] A man is not learned because he talks much; he who is patient, free from hatred and fear, he is called learned.

We cannot distinguish whether a person is learned or not when they are completely silent. It's when someone opens their mouth, we begin to see whether they are wise and righteous or foolish. However, talking too much, making idle chatter, venting every feeling and thought a person has, this does not describe a learned person. We ought to avoid idle, unrestrained chatter.

---

[453] Proverbs 10:19 (AMP).
[454] Proverbs 29:11 (NKJV).
[455] Proverbs 14:23b (NKJV).

Day 223

Solomon

Buddha

The mouth of the righteous man utters wisdom, and his tongue speaks what is just. The law of his God is in his heart; his feet do not slip.[456]

[259] A man is not a supporter of the law because he talks much; even if a man has learnt little, but sees the law bodily, he is a supporter of the law, a man who never neglects the law.

If we are attentive to studying the law and living by it, our speech will be seasoned and restrained, and we will speak with wisdom and discretion. If the law is in our hearts, we will not slip and fall. King David wrote:

> How blessed are those whose way is blameless, who walk in the law of the LORD. How blessed are those who observe His testimonies [law], who seek Him with all their heart. They also do no unrighteousness; they walk in His ways. [457]

---

[456] Psalm 37:30-31 (NIV), a psalm of King David, Solomon's father.
[457] Psalm 119:1-3 (NASB).

Day 224

Solomon

Buddha

Better a poor but wise youth than an old but foolish king who no longer knows how to take warning.[458]

[260] A man is not an elder because his head is grey; his age may be ripe, but he is called "Old-in-vain."

We cannot judge the wisdom of someone else based on their age, and we cannot assume that as we age we will naturally become wise. One can be old and foolish at the same time, just as someone young can be foolish. One element of being wise is knowing how to accept a legitimate warning with humility.

---

[458] Ecclesiastes 4:13 (NIV).

Day 225

Solomon

He who deals wisely and heeds [God's] word and counsel shall find good, and whoever leans on, trusts in, and is confident in the Lord—happy, blessed, and fortunate is he. The wise in heart are called prudent, understanding, and knowing, and winsome speech increases learning [in both speaker and listener].[459]

Wisdom makes one wise man more powerful than ten rulers in a city.[460]

Buddha

[261] He in whom there is truth, virtue, love, restraint, moderation, he who is free from impurity and is wise, he is called an elder.

When we heed instruction and the law, filling our lives with truth, virtue, love, restraint, moderation, and we are free from impurity, we are wise. Better is wisdom than the power of many politicians or rulers.

---

[459] Proverbs 16:20-21 (AMP).
[460] Ecclesiastes 7:19 (NIV).

Day 226

Solomon

Buddha

The wise of heart will receive commands, but a babbling fool will be ruined. He who walks in integrity walks securely, but he who perverts his ways will be found out. He who winks the eye causes trouble, and a babbling fool will be ruined. The mouth of the righteous is a fountain of life, but the mouth of the wicked conceals violence.[461]

[262] An envious greedy, dishonest man does not become respectable by means of much talking only, or by the beauty of his complexion.

Smooth talking and good looks cannot make up for being envious or greedy. Over time, our speech reveals our hearts. Out of a violent heart comes violent speech. We ought to be people of integrity, being whole and honest, and having a sound moral character.

---

[461] Proverbs 10:8-11 (NASB).

Day 227

Solomon

Hatred stirs up strife, but love covers all sins.[462]

Better is a dish of vegetables where love is than a fattened ox served with hatred.[463]

Buddha

[263] He in whom all this is destroyed, and taken out with the very root, he, when freed from hatred and wise, is called respectable.

Hatred breeds dissension. Even the wealthiest home when filled with hatred is not a pleasant place to live. Better to have only a plate of vegetables to eat where there is love, than to be a wealthy person with the finest food to eat and be full of hate.

---

[462] Proverbs 10:12 (NKJV).
[463] Proverbs 15:17 (NASB).

Day 228

Solomon	Buddha

Buy the truth and do not sell it; get wisdom, discipline and understanding.[464]

The righteousness of the upright will deliver them, but the treacherous will be caught by their own greed.[465]

[264] Not by tonsure [shaving one's head] does an undisciplined man who speaks falsehood become a Samana; can a man be a Samana who is still held captive by desire and greediness?

Desire and greed capture the undisciplined. Outward manifestations of discipline are not enough if we are already captive. Obtaining truth, wisdom, discipline and understanding delivers us from an undisciplined life.

---

[464] Proverbs 23:23 (NIV).
[465] Proverbs 11:6 (NASB).

Day 229

Solomon

Do not be wise in your own eyes; fear the LORD and depart from evil.[466]

A wise man is cautious and turns away from evil, but a fool is arrogant and careless.[467]

But he who listens to me [wisdom] shall live securely and will be at ease from the dread of evil.[468]

Buddha

[265] He who always quiets the evil, whether small or large, he is called a Samana (a quiet man), because he has quieted all evil.

Quieting, shunning and departing from evil is a wise path. Being attentive to wisdom creates a secure life, free from the dread of evil. We ought not to let pride detour us. Seeking after wisdom quiets evil.

---

[466] Proverbs 3:7 (NKJV).
[467] Proverbs 14:16 (NASB).
[468] Proverbs 1:33 (NASB).

Day 230

Solomon	Buddha

Receive my instruction [wisdom's], and not silver, and knowledge rather than choice gold; for wisdom is better than rubies, and all the things one may desire cannot be compared with her.[469]

The mind of the prudent acquires knowledge, and the ear of the wise seeks knowledge.[470]

266 A man is not a mendicant (Bhikshu) simply because he asks others for alms; he who adopts the whole law is a Bhikshu, not he who only begs.

267 He who is above good and evil, who is chaste, who with knowledge passes through the world, he indeed is called a Bhikshu.

Outward appearances or deeds do not make us righteous, and acquiring wealth does not make us wise. Better to be discerning, prudent and chaste and seek after wisdom and knowledge by embracing the whole law.

---

[469] Proverbs 8:10-11 (NKJV).
[470] Proverbs 18:15 (NASB).

Day 231

Solomon

Good judgment wins favor,
but the way of the unfaithful
leads to their destruction.[471]

The heart of the righteous
weighs its answers, but the
mouth of the wicked gushes
evil.[472]

Buddha

[268, 269.] A man is not a Muni
[holy person or sage]
because he observes silence
(mona, i.e. mauna), if he is
foolish and ignorant; but
the wise who, taking the
balance, chooses the good
and avoids evil, he is a
Muni, and is a Muni
thereby; he who in this
world weighs both sides is
called a Muni.

Avoiding or turning away from evil is wise. Examining a situation and weighing the consequences of doing good or doing evil, the wise will choose good.

---

[471] Proverbs 13:15 (NIV).
[472] Proverbs 15:28 (NIV).

Day 232

Solomon

A righteous man cares for the needs of his animal, but the kindest acts of the wicked are cruel.[473]

Be diligent to know the state of your flocks, and attend to your herds; for riches are not forever, nor does a crown endure to all generations. When the hay is removed, and the tender grass shows itself, and the herbs of the mountains are gathered in, the lambs will provide your clothing, and the goats the price of a field; you shall have enough goats' milk for your food, for the food of your household, and the nourishment of your maidservants.[474]

Buddha

[270] A man is not an elect (Ariya) because he injures living creatures; because he has pity on all living creatures, therefore is a man called Ariya.

Caring for one's pets or livestock and having kindness and pity toward animals is a distinguishing trait of the righteous.

---

[473] Proverbs 12:10 (NIV).
[474] Proverbs 27:23–27 (NKJV).

Day 233

Solomon

Buddha

The righteousness of the upright [their rectitude in every area and relation] shall deliver them, but the treacherous shall be taken in their own iniquity and greedy desire.[475]

The wicked desire the plunder of evil men, but the root of the righteous flourishes.[476]

[271, 272.] Not only by discipline and vows, not only by much learning, not by entering into a trance, not by sleeping alone, do I earn the happiness of release which no worldling [sic] can know. Bhikshu, be not confident as long as thou hast not attained the extinction of desires.

We have no hope of living a righteous life if our desires rule us. Trapped by them, we will be tossed about by every whim we have. Even jumping through the hoops of living a righteous life by exerting various disciplines upon ourselves will not succeed in prevailing over unrestrained desires.

---

[475] Proverbs 11:6 (AMP).
[476] Proverbs 12:12 (NIV).

Chapter Twenty – The Way

(Days 234-246, Dhammapada 273-289)

Chapter Twenty discusses the way (path) to living a righteous life. It is the way of wisdom, and of having moral and spiritual virtue.

Walking the path of wisdom, we are freed from the painful results of evil.

When we rouse ourselves to be diligent in our mind, will, body, and daily work, and remember to be generous with what we have, this assists us in living a righteous life.

Day 234

Solomon (950 BCE)

Buddha (525 BCE)

My fruit is better than gold, yes, than refined gold, and my increase than choice silver. I [Wisdom] walk in the way of righteousness (moral and spiritual rectitude in every area and relation), in the midst of the paths of justice, that I may cause those who love me to inherit [true] riches and that I may fill their treasuries.[477]

273 The best of ways is the eightfold; the best of truths the four words; the best of virtues passionlessness; the best of men he who has eyes to see.

274 This is the way, there is no other that leads to the purifying of intelligence. Go on this way! Everything else is the deceit of Mara (the tempter).

The best of ways is the way of wisdom. Having moral and spiritual virtue (rightness of principle and conduct) assists us in that path. The path of wisdom fills us with true riches.

---

477 Proverbs 8:19-21 (AMP).

Day 235

Solomon	**Buddha**

The highway of the upright avoids evil; he who guards his way guards his life.[478]

[275] If you go on this way, you will make an end of pain! The way was preached by me, when I had understood the removal of the thorns (in the flesh).

If we go the way of wisdom, we are freed from walking the thorny, painful paths of evil. The way of wisdom prepares a straight path for us where we are not hampered and we will not stumble.

---

[478] Proverbs 16:17 (NIV).

Day 236

Solomon

Buddha

Listen, my son, accept what I say, and the years of your life will be many. I guide you in the way of wisdom and lead you along straight paths. When you walk, your steps will not be hampered; when you run, you will not stumble. Hold on to instruction, do not let it go; guard it well, for it is your life. Do not set foot on the path of the wicked or walk in the way of evil men. Avoid it, do not travel on it; turn from it and go on your way.[479]

[276] You yourself must make an effort. The Tathagatas (Buddhas) are only preachers. The thoughtful who enter the way are freed from the bondage of Mara.

Living mindfully allows us to choose a righteous path and avoid the snares and pitfalls of doing evil. Hold on to knowledge and wisdom and avoid evil.

---

[479] Proverbs 4:10-15 (NIV).

Day 237

Solomon

Buddha

As he came from his mother's womb, naked shall he return, to go as he came; and he shall take nothing from his labor which he may carry away in his hand. And this also is a severe evil—just exactly as he came, so shall he go.[480]

[277] 'All created things perish,' he who knows and sees this becomes passive in pain; this is the way to purity

We are wise to remember that all perish, and as we were born, so shall we leave this world and take nothing we have earned or owned in this life with us. Naked we are born and naked we shall go.

Day 238

Solomon

Buddha

And what profit has he who has labored for the wind? All his days he also eats in darkness, and he has much sorrow and sickness and anger.[481]

[278] 'All created things are grief and pain,' he who knows and sees this becomes passive in pain; this is the way that leads to purity.

Everyone experiences pain in this lifetime. No one is exempt. This knowledge can lead us to compassion for our fellow man.

---

[480] Ecclesiastes 5:15–16a (NKJV).
[481] Ecclesiastes 5:16–17 (NKJV).

Day 239

Solomon

Buddha

"Meaningless! Meaningless!" says the Teacher. "Utterly meaningless! Everything is meaningless."[482]

[279] 'All forms are unreal,' he who knows and sees this becomes passive in pain; this is the way that leads to purity.

What we think is the true nature of things isn't real. It is all an illusion. Realizing this helps us to stop desiring most things in this life.

---

[482] Ecclesiastes 1:2 (NIV).

Day 240

| Solomon | Buddha |

He who is slothful in his work is a brother to him who is a great destroyer.[483]

In the house of the wise are stores of choice food and oil, but a foolish man devours all he has. . . . The sluggard's craving will be the death of him, because his hands refuse to work. All day long he craves for more, but the righteous give without sparing.[484]

[280] He who does not rouse himself when it is time to rise, who, though young and strong, is full of sloth, whose will and thought are weak, that lazy and idle man will never find the way to knowledge.

Sloth does not lead to knowledge, and sloth in work can destroy a life. We ought to rouse ourselves to diligence in our mind, will, body and daily work, while remembering to be generous with what we have.

---

[483] Proverbs 18:9 (NKJV).
[484] Proverbs 21:20, 25-26 (NIV).

Day 241

Solomon

He who loves a pure heart and whose speech is gracious will have the king for his friend.[485]

A man will be praised according to his insight, but one of perverse mind will be despised.[486]

Do not be wise in your own eyes; fear the LORD and shun evil. This will bring health to your body and nourishment to your bones.[487]

Buddha

[281] Watching his speech, well restrained in mind, let a man never commit any wrong with his body! Let a man but keep these three roads of action clear, and he will achieve the way which is taught by the wise.

Avoiding evil and being restrained in our thought life, guarding our speech, and disciplining our bodies are three areas of our lives we should focus on. By having self discipline in these areas, we can see immediate benefits, such as health and purity.

---

[485] Proverbs 22:11 (NIV).
[486] Proverbs 12:8 (NASB).
[487] Proverbs 3:7-8 (NIV).

Day 242

Solomon

Get wisdom! Get understanding! Do not forget, nor turn away from the words of my mouth. Do not forsake her, and she will preserve you; Love her, and she will keep you. Wisdom is the principal thing; therefore get wisdom. And in all your getting, get understanding. Exalt her, and she will promote you; she will bring you honor, when you embrace her.[488]

Choose my [Wisdom's] instruction instead of silver, knowledge rather than choice gold, for wisdom is more precious than rubies, and nothing you desire can compare with her.[489]

Buddha

[282] Through zeal knowledge is gotten, through lack of zeal knowledge is lost; let a man who knows this double path of gain and loss thus place himself that knowledge may grow.

Knowledge is obtained by choosing to be zealous and passionate about learning, and being diligent in our studies. Wisdom and knowledge are more precious than gold, silver or jewels. Let us be zealous! Get wisdom! Get understanding!

---

[488] Proverbs 4:5–8 (NKJV).
[489] Proverbs 8:10–11 (NIV).

Day 243

Solomon

Do not lust in your heart after her beauty or let her captivate you with her eyes, for the prostitute reduces you to a loaf of bread, and the adulteress preys upon your very life. Can a man scoop fire into his lap without his clothes being burned? Can a man walk on hot coals without his feet being scorched? So is he who sleeps with another man's wife; no one who touches her will go unpunished.[490]

Buddha

[283] Cut down the whole forest (of lust), not a tree only! Danger comes out of the forest (of lust). When you have cut down both the forest (of lust) and its undergrowth, then, Bhikshus, you will be rid of the forest and free!

[284] So long as the love of man towards women, even the smallest, is not destroyed, so long is his mind in bondage, as the calf that drinks milk is to its mother.

Danger results from lust. Seeking after a prostitute or having an adulterous affair can result in disaster, publicly and privately, even to the point of compromising our health and costing lives.

---

[490] Proverbs 6:25-29 (NIV).

Day 244

Solomon

Buddha

An unfriendly man pursues selfish ends; he defies all sound judgment. A fool finds no pleasure in understanding but delights in airing his own opinions.[491]

There is deceit in the hearts of those who plot evil, but joy for those who promote peace.[492]

[285] Cut out the love of self, like an autumn lotus, with thy hand! Cherish the road of peace. Nirvana has been shown by Sugata (Buddha).

If we blindly and selfishly go through life only caring about our own needs, wants and opinions, we will not create peace. We will only generate conflict. We ought to cut out selfishness and cherish peace.

---

[491] Proverbs 18:1-2 (NIV).
[492] Proverbs 12:20 (NIV).

Day 245

Solomon

Buddha

A good name is better than precious ointment, and the day of death than the day of one's birth; better to go to the house of mourning than to go to the house of feasting, for that is the end of all men; and the living will take it to heart.[493]

[286] 'Here I shall dwell in the rain, here in winter and summer,' thus the fool meditates, and does not think of his death.

[287] Death comes and carries off that man, praised for his children and flocks, his mind distracted, as a flood carries off a sleeping village.

Remembering that we all die, keeps us sober as we think about our lives and how to spend them. Otherwise, we can get caught up in false thinking about what's important. We can find ourselves saying that we'll go here and do this and that, and before we know it our lives have come to an end. Better to live mindfully and with purpose for we do not know when we shall die.

---

[493] Ecclesiastes 7:1-2 (NKJV).

Day 246

Solomon

For who knows what is good for a man in life, during the few and meaningless days he passes through like a shadow? Who can tell him what will happen under the sun after he is gone?[494]

Buddha

[288] Sons are no help, nor a father, nor relations; there is no help from kinsfolk for one whom death has seized.

[289] A wise and good man who knows the meaning of this, should quickly clear the way that leads to Nirvana.

Once we are dead, our family cannot help us, and we do not have control over what we have left behind. We can only control our decisions while we are alive.

---

[494] Ecclesiastes 6:12 (NIV).

Chapter Twenty-One – Miscellaneous

(Days 247-260, Dhammapada 290-305)

This chapter contains proverbs on a variety of topics, such as the problem of clinging to things that we think are good for us, while missing what is better; replacing cruelty and anger with self-control; choosing watchfulness and mindfulness over sloth; and knowing our actions emanate from our thoughts and thus keeping guard over them.

Mindfully avoiding evil is health and nourishment to our bodies, and delighting in compassion, kindness and generosity are encouraged.

Day 247

Solomon (950 BCE)

Buddha (525 BCE)

The desire of the lazy [slothful] man kills him, for his hands refuse to labor. He covets greedily all day long, but the righteous gives and does not spare.[495]

[290] If by leaving a small pleasure one sees a great pleasure, let a wise man leave the small pleasure, and look to the great.

We can become myopic, coveting and clinging to things that we think are good for us, while missing that which is better for us. We ought to let go of coveting and clinging, and seek the better path of being generous and unselfish.

---

[495] Proverbs 21:25–26 (NKJV).

Day 248

Solomon

The merciful, kind, and generous man benefits himself [for his deeds return to bless him], but he who is cruel and callous [to the wants of others] brings on himself retribution.[496]

He who is slow to anger is better than the mighty. And he who rules his spirit than he who takes a city.[497]

Buddha

[291] He who, by causing pain to others, wishes to obtain pleasure for himself, he, entangled in the bonds of hatred, will never be free from hatred.

Being cruel, angry or hateful brings us under bondage, and brings retribution back upon us. Better to have self-control, and be merciful, kind and generous.

---

[496] Proverbs 11:17 (AMP).
[497] Proverbs 16:32 (NKJV).

Day 249

Solomon

A simple man believes anything, but a prudent man gives thought to his steps. A wise man fears the LORD and shuns evil, but a fool is hotheaded and reckless.[498]

Buddha

[292] What ought to be done is neglected, what ought not to be done is done; the desires of unruly, thoughtless people are always increasing.

There is a struggle within us each day to choose between doing right and good, and doing evil. The Apostle Paul describes this battle at length in Romans 7. In verse 15 he writes,

> For I do not understand my own actions [I am baffled, bewildered]. I do not practice or accomplish what I wish, but I do the very thing that I loathe [which my moral instinct condemns].[499]

If we wish to do the good and right thing, we must fight against the inclination to do something not good every day.

---

[498] Proverbs 14:15-16 (NIV).
[499] Romans 7:15 (AMP).

Day 250

Solomon

Buddha

Do not those who plot evil go astray? But those who plan what is good find love and faithfulness.[500]

I know that there is nothing better for them, than to rejoice, and to do good so long as they live.[501]

[293] But they whose whole watchfulness is always directed to their body, who do not follow what ought not to be done, and who steadfastly do what ought to be done, the desires of such watchful and wise people will come to an end.

Doing the right thing means being proactive. It means being watchful, wise and planning to do good, not sitting back and letting our baser desires propel us through each day. King David knew this and wrote,

Depart from evil and do good; seek peace and pursue it.[502]

---

[500] Proverbs 14:22 (NIV).
[501] Ecclesiastes 3:12 (ASV).
[502] Psalm 34:14 (NKJV), a psalm of King David, Solomon's father.

Day 251

Solomon

A time to kill and a time to heal; a time to tear down and a time to build up.[503]

Buddha

[294] A true Brahmana goes scatheless, though he have killed father and mother, and two valiant kings, though he has destroyed a kingdom with all its subjects.

[295] A true Brahmana goes scatheless, though he have killed father and mother, and two holy kings, and an eminent man besides.

Tragically, there are times when it is appropriate to kill someone or destroy a town. Murder and destruction ought to be avoided, but there are times when it cannot, such as defending your loved ones from attack or your home against invasion. And there are times when it is right and just to come to another person's rescue.

---

[503] Ecclesiastes 3:3 (NASB).

Day 252

Solomon	Buddha

Trust in the LORD with all your heart, and lean not on your own understanding; in all your ways acknowledge Him, and He shall direct your paths.[504]

O how I love Your law! It is my meditation all the day.[505]

[296] The disciples of Gotama (Buddha) are always well awake, and their thoughts day and night are always set on Buddha.

[297] The disciples of Gotama are always well awake, and their thoughts day and night are always set on the law.

Our thoughts should always be focused on the Lord, or on his law, clearly affecting everything we do or say. This will bring nourishment to our minds and souls. For what our thoughts rest upon, so shall our actions emanate from. What we value and treasure will be revealed in the way we conduct our lives.

---

[504] Proverbs 3:5-6 (NKJV).
[505] Psalm 119:97 (NASB).

Day 253

Solomon	Buddha
For a day in Your courts is better than a thousand [anywhere else]; I would rather be a doorkeeper and stand at the threshold in the house of my God than to dwell [at ease] in the tents of wickedness.[506]	[298] The disciples of Gotama are always well awake, and their thoughts day and night are always set on the church.

Having our thoughts set on the church and serving in the church for a single day is far better than spending a thousand days anywhere else. Better to serve in a lowly position in the church, than to live comfortably among wayward people.

Day 254

Solomon	Buddha
The one who gets wisdom loves life; the one who cherishes understanding will soon prosper.[507]	[299] The disciples of Gotama are always well awake, and their thoughts day and night are always set on their body.

Mindfully avoiding evil is health and nourishment to our bodies. Choosing to do good and right things with our bodies is a wise things to do. The alternative invites illness and misfortune.

---

[506] Psalm 84:10 (AMP).
[507] Proverbs 19:8 (NIV).

Day 255

Solomon

He who despises his neighbor sins [against God, his fellowman, and himself], but happy (blessed and fortunate) is he who is kind and merciful to the poor.[508]

A generous man will prosper; he who refreshes others will himself be refreshed.[509]

Buddha

[300] The disciples of Gotama are always well awake, and their mind day and night always delights in compassion.

Delight in compassion, kindness and generosity. Thinking of others and being generous of heart and with our material means is refreshing to our souls.

---

[508] Proverbs 14:21 (AMP).
[509] Proverbs 11:25 (NIV).

Day 256

Solomon

Buddha

But his delight is in the law of the LORD, and on his law he meditates day and night.[510]

Within your temple, O God, we meditate on your unfailing love.[511]

I lift up my hands to your commands, which I love, and I meditate on your decrees.[512]

Oh, how I love your law! I meditate on it all day long.[513]

[301] The disciples of Gotama are always well awake, and their mind day and night always delights in meditation.

Delighting in the law and in meditation, and being mindful of our thoughts and actions is the path of wisdom.

---

[510] Psalm 1:2 (NIV), a psalm of King David, Solomon's father.
[511] Psalm 48:9 (NIV), a psalm of King David, Solomon's father.
[512] Psalm 119:48 (NIV).
[513] Psalm 119:97 (NIV).

Day 257

Solomon

Buddha

All things are weary with toil and all words are feeble; man cannot utter it. The eye is not satisfied with seeing, nor the ear filled with hearing.[514]

[302] It is hard to leave the world (to become a friar), it is hard to enjoy the world; hard is the monastery, painful are the houses; painful it is to dwell with equals (to share everything in common) and the itinerant mendicant is beset with pain. Therefore let no man be an itinerant mendicant and he will not be beset with pain.

Whether we live in a monastery or in a fine home, life is difficult and fraught with pain. Most difficult of all is the life of the wandering beggar. If we let our desires run wild, they will never be satisfied.

---

[514] Ecclesiastes 1:8 (AMP).

Day 258

Solomon

Buddha

When the righteous prosper, the city rejoices; when the wicked perish, there are shouts of joy.[515]

The wicked are overthrown and are no more, but the house of the righteous will stand.[516]

[303] Whatever place a faithful, virtuous, celebrated, and wealthy man chooses, there he is respected.

A faithful, virtuous person is celebrated and respected wherever they live. When we are faithful and virtuous, our behavior benefits all those around us. We may not be aware of it, but our behavior and choices have an impact. Let us be mindful of our choices.

---

[515] Proverbs 11:10 (NIV).
[516] Proverbs 12:7 (NASB).

Day 259

Solomon

The light of the [uncom-
promisingly] righteous [is
within him—it grows brighter
and] rejoices, but the lamp of
the wicked [furnishes only a
derived, temporary light and]
shall be put out shortly.[517]

Buddha

[301] Good people shine from
afar, like the snowy
mountains; bad people are
not seen, like arrows shot
by night.

Righteous people shine like snow-topped mountains. Their
light continues to shine and grow brighter. Whatever light the
wicked once had is extinguished. Like trying to shoot an arrow at
a target in darkness, it misses the mark. Let goodness shine
brightly in our lives.

Day 260

Solomon

Better to live on a corner of
the roof than share a house
with a quarrelsome wife.[518]

Buddha

[305] He alone who, without
ceasing, practises [sic] the
duty of sitting alone and
sleeping alone, he, subduing
himself, will rejoice in the
destruction of all desires
alone, as if living in a forest.

There are virtues to solitude, and one is that we can focus all
our attention on self-control.

---

[517] Proverbs 13:9 (AMP).
[518] Proverbs 21:9 (NIV).

Chapter Twenty-Two –

The Downward Course

(Days 261-272, Dhammapada 306-319)

This chapter describes ways to avoid the downward course into evil behavior. Allowing small evils to creep into our lives can lead to us to greater offenses. Consider, we often make a distinction between telling a white lie, boldly lying and committing perjury. Rather than making distinctions between small deceits and bold ones, we ought to conduct ourselves with integrity, and avoid the downward course.

Allowing momentary lust to lead to adultery is another example of the downward course.

Even in practicing austerity and self-denial, let us not allow pride to creep in. Like a soldier guarding a fort, we ought to take great care to guard ourselves from evil.

Day 261

Solomon (950 BCE)

There are six things the LORD hates, seven that are detestable to him: haughty eyes, a lying tongue, hands that shed innocent blood, a heart that devises wicked schemes, feet that are quick to rush into evil, a false witness who pours out lies and a man who stirs up dissension among brothers.[519]

A false witness will not go unpunished, and he who speaks lies shall perish.[520]

Buddha (525 BCE)

[306] He who says what is not, goes to hell; he also who, having done a thing, says I have not done it. After death both are equal, they are men with evil deeds in the next world.

Human as we are, we tend to make distinctions between telling white lies, boldly lying, and committing perjury. After all, one can land you in jail. But spiritually there is no distinction. Rather than making distinctions and rationalizing our behavior, if we speak the truth at all times that is the best solution, and it's much easier to remember.

---

[519] Proverbs 6:16-19 (NIV).
[520] Proverbs 19:9 (NKJV).

Day 262

Solomon	Buddha
The truly righteous man attains life, but he who pursues evil goes to his death.[521]	[307] Many men whose shoulders are covered with the yellow gown are ill-conditioned and unrestrained; such evil-doers by their evil deeds go to hell.
He who heeds discipline shows the way to life, but whoever ignores correction leads others astray.[522]	
He who neglects discipline despises himself, but he who listens to reproof acquires understanding.[523]	

Those who are undisciplined and unrestrained lead others astray, bring ruin upon themselves, and even can bring their own death. We would be wise to choose discipline and righteousness, otherwise our unrestrained behavior shows we despise ourselves.

---

[521] Proverbs 11:19 (NIV).
[522] Proverbs 10:17 (NIV).
[523] Proverbs 15:32 (NASB).

Day 263

Solomon

Buddha

Bread gained by deceit is sweet to a man, but afterward his mouth will be filled with gravel.[524]

In the house of the wise are stores of choice food and oil, but a foolish man devours all he has.[525]

[308] Better it would be to swallow a heated iron ball, like flaring fire, than that a bad unrestrained fellow should live on the charity of the land.

It is better for us to work hard and be able to give to those genuinely in need, than to be capable of work but lazy and receive charity. Our deceit would change the ill-gotten food to gravel in our mouths.

---

[524] Proverbs 20:17 (NKJV).
[525] Proverbs 21:20 (NIV).

Day 264

Solomon

Buddha

Why be captivated, my son, by an adulteress? Why embrace the bosom of another man's wife? For a man's ways are in full view of the LORD, and he examines all his paths. The evil deeds of a wicked man ensnare him; the cords of his sin hold him fast. He will die for lack of discipline, led astray by his own great folly.[526]

[309] Four things does a wreckless [sic] man gain who covets his neighbour's [sic] wife,—a bad reputation, an uncomfortable bed, thirdly, punishment, and lastly, hell.

Adultery is a snare resulting in ruined reputations and destroyed families and lives. It is a great folly hurting many people. Better to have integrity and live faithful lives, not coveting someone else's spouse. In the Ten Commandments it reads,

> You shall not covet your neighbor's house; you shall not covet your neighbor's wife or his male servant or his female servant or his ox or his donkey or anything that belongs to your neighbor.[527]

---

[526] Proverbs 5:20-23 (NIV).
[527] Exodus 20:17 (NASB). Moses lived at least 200 years prior to Solomon.

Day 265

Solomon

Let your fountain be blessed, and rejoice in the wife of your youth. As a loving hind and a graceful doe, let her breasts satisfy you at all times; be exhilarated always with her love. For why should you, my son, be exhilarated with an adulteress and embrace the bosom of a foreigner?[528]

Buddha

[310] There is bad reputation, and the evil way (to hell), there is the short pleasure of the frightened in the arms of the frightened, and the king imposes heavy punishment; therefore let no man think of his neighbour's [*sic*] wife.

Adultery begins with the thought life. If we keep our thoughts on our own spouse, we will not stray. Rejoice in your own spouse and do not give room for any thought of another's.

---

[528] Proverbs 5:18-20 (NASB).

Day 266

Solomon

Buddha

There is a way that appears
to be right, but in the end it
leads to death.[529]

Like a city whose walls are
broken down is a man who
lacks self-control.[530]

[311] As a grass-blade, if badly
grasped, cuts the arm, badly-
practised [sic] asceticism
leads to hell.

Even in practicing self-denial and austerity, we ought to be
mindful of not straying from wisdom and knowledge, otherwise
we might think we are living righteously, but we would really be
living in error and pride.

---

[529] Proverbs 16:25 (NIV).
[530] Proverbs 25:28 (NIV).

Day 267

Solomon	Buddha
When you make a vow to God, do not be late in paying it; for He takes no delight in fools. Pay what you vow! It is better that you should not vow than that you should vow and not pay. Do not let your speech cause you to sin and do not say in the presence of the messenger of God that it was a mistake. Why should God be angry on account of your voice and destroy the work of your hands?[531]	[312] An act carelessly performed, a broken vow, and hesitating obedience to discipline, all this brings no great reward.

We ought to be very careful about vowing or making promises. Our words carry weight, and if we do not follow through it destroys our integrity and credibility.

---

[531] Ecclesiastes 5:4-6 (NASB).

Day 268

Solomon

Whatever your hand finds to
do, do it with all your might,
for in the realm of the dead,
where you are going, there is
neither working nor planning
nor knowledge nor
wisdom.[532]

Fools fold their hands and
ruin themselves.[533]

Buddha

[313] If anything is to be done,
let a man do it, let him
attack it vigorously! A
careless pilgrim only scatters
the dust of his passions
more widely.

Let us find joy in our work and do it diligently, for only a
foolish, careless person sits back and allows desires and passions
to lead them astray and ruin their lives.

---

[532] Ecclesiastes 9:10 (NIV).
[533] Ecclesiastes 4:5 (NIV).

Day 269

Solomon

For God will bring every work into judgment, including every secret thing, whether good or evil.[534]

Do they not err who devise evil and wander from the way of life? But loving-kindness and mercy, loyalty and faithfulness, shall be to those who devise good.[535]

The faithless will be fully repaid for their ways, and the good man rewarded for his.[536]

Buddha

[314] An evil deed is better left undone, for a man repents of it afterwards; a good deed is better done, for having done it, one does not repent.

Leave evil deeds undone, and pursue doing good deeds. For all deeds come to light and are repaid in this life or the next. As far as it is in our power, let us do good. In Psalms we read,

> Depart from evil and do good; seek peace and pursue it.[537] Good will come to him who is generous and lends freely, who conducts his affairs with justice.[538]

---

[534] Ecclesiastes 12:14 (NKJV).
[535] Proverbs 14:22 (AMP).
[536] Proverbs 14:14 (NIV).
[537] Psalm 34:14 (NASB), a psalm of King David, Solomon's father.
[538] Psalm 112:5 (NIV).

Day 270

Solomon

Buddha

The highway of the upright turns aside from evil; he who guards his way preserves his life.[539]

He who obeys instructions guards his life, but he who is contemptuous of his ways will die.[540]

[315] Like a well-guarded frontier fort, with defences [*sic*] within and without, so let a man guard himself. Not a moment should escape, for they who allow the right moment to pass, suffer pain when they are in hell.

Like a soldier guarding a fort, we ought to take great care to guard ourselves from evil. By doing so, we guard ourselves from harm. Buddha taught not to let a moment pass by without guarding ourselves.

---

[539] Proverbs 16:17 (AMP).
[540] Proverbs 19:16 (NIV).

Day 271

Solomon	Buddha
A truthful witness saves lives, but a deceitful witness speaks lies [and endangers lives].[541]	[316] They who are ashamed of what they ought not to be ashamed of, and are not ashamed of what they ought to be ashamed of, such men, embracing false doctrines enter the evil path.
A man who bears false witness against his neighbor is like a club, a sword, and a sharp arrow.[542]	[317] They who fear when they ought not to fear, and fear not when they ought to fear, such men, embracing false doctrines, enter the evil path.

It is useless to be ashamed of or to fear a behavior that is good, or not to be ashamed or not to fear a behavior that is bad. Being able to discern between good and evil and knowing how to live honestly and speak truthfully are abilities and behaviors to be cultivated. The alternative leads to an evil path.

---

[541] Proverbs 14:25 (AMP).
[542] Proverbs 25:18 (NKJV).

Day 272

Solomon

A [consistently] righteous man hates lying and deceit, but a wicked man is loathsome [his very breath spreads pollution] and he comes [surely] to shame.[543]

There is deceit in the hearts of those who plot evil, but joy for those who promote peace.[544]

Lying lips are an abomination to the LORD, but those who deal truthfully are His delight.[545]

Buddha

[318] They who forbid when there is nothing to be forbidden, and forbid not when there is something to be forbidden, such men, embracing false doctrines, enter the evil path.

[319] They who know what is forbidden as forbidden, and what is not forbidden as not forbidden, such men, embracing the true doctrine, enter the good path.

Deception and manipulation ought never to be our way, for the righteous hate lying. Let us promote truth and peace in every facet of our lives.

---

[543] Proverbs 13:5 (AMP).
[544] Proverbs 12:20 (NIV).
[545] Proverbs 12:22 (NKJV).

Chapter Twenty-Three – The Elephant

(Days 273-283, Dhammapada 320-333)

This chapter uses examples drawn from the animal kingdom to discuss the righteous life.

For example, the tamed elephant in a battle will endure abuse silently, as we are encouraged to overlook insults and offenses by returning and promoting love, and like an elephant sunk in mud must draw himself out we are to draw ourselves out of the evil way.

Making a habit of living mindfully and giving thought to our actions makes this easier over time.

Day 273

Solomon (950 BCE)

A fool shows his annoyance at once, but a prudent man overlooks an insult.[546]

He who covers a transgression seeks love, but he who repeats a matter separates friends.[547]

Buddha (525 BCE)

[320] Silently shall I endure abuse as the elephant in battle endures the arrow sent from the bow: for the world is ill-natured.

When we overlook insults and offenses, we promote love. The Apostle Peter wrote, "Above all, keep fervent in your love for one another, because love covers a multitude of sins."[548]

---

[546] Proverbs 12:16 (NIV).
[547] Proverbs 17:9 (NKJV).
[548] 1 Peter 4:8 (NASB).

Day 274

Solomon	Buddha

Whoever corrects a mocker invites insult; whoever rebukes a wicked man incurs abuse.[549]

Better a patient person than a warrior, one with self-control than one who takes a city.[550]

[321] They lead a tamed elephant to battle, the king mounts a tamed elephant; the tamed is the best among men, he who silently endures abuse.

Better to be patient and have self-control (be tamed), than to incite abuse. We cannot control others, we can only discipline ourselves. We have a choice regarding how we will respond to someone who is insulting or abusive. We can still be at peace regardless of the actions of others. Kind David wrote,

> Be still and rest in the Lord; wait for Him and patiently lean yourself upon Him; fret not yourself because of him who prospers in his way, because of the man who brings wicked devices to pass.[551]

---

[549] Proverbs 9:7 (NIV).
[550] Proverbs 16:32 (NIV).
[551] Psalm 37:7 (AMP), a psalm of King David, Solomon's father.

293

Day 275

Solomon	Buddha

Solomon

He who is slow to anger is better than the mighty, he who rules his [own] spirit than he who takes a city.[552]

Buddha

322 Mules are good, if tamed, and noble Sindhu horses, and elephants with large tusks; but he who tames himself is better still.

323 For with these animals does no man reach the untrodden country (Nirvana), where a tamed man goes on a tamed animal, viz. on his own well-tamed self.

If we tame ourselves with discipline and self-control, we are better than a mighty warrior who can take a city, or a beast of burden who has been domesticated.

---

[552] Proverbs 16:32 (AMP).

Day 276

Solomon

Buddha

May those who hope in you not be disgraced because of me, O Lord, the LORD Almighty; may those who seek you not be put to shame because of me, O God of Israel. For I endure scorn for your sake, and shame covers my face. I am a stranger to my brothers, an alien to my own mother's sons; for zeal for your house consumes me, and the insults of those who insult you fall on me. When I weep and fast, I must endure scorn; when I put on sackcloth, people make sport of me. Those who sit at the gate mock me, and I am the song of the drunkards.[553]

324 The elephant called Dhanapalaka, his temples running with sap, and difficult to hold, does not eat a morsel when bound; the elephant longs for the elephant grove.

When we are heartbroken and can't see any way to escape a sorrowful, difficult situation, we most long to rise above it and exist in a peaceful, safe place. At such a time, let us be persistent in our studies and meditation.

---

[553] Psalm 69:6-12 (NIV), a psalm of King David, Solomon's father.

Day 277

Solomon

When you sit to dine with a ruler, note well what is before you, and put a knife to your throat if you are given to gluttony. Do not crave his delicacies, for that food is deceptive.[554]

Hear, my son, and be wise; and guide your heart in the way. Do not mix with winebibbers, or with gluttonous eaters of meat; for the drunkard and the glutton will come to poverty, and drowsiness will clothe a man with rags.[555]

Buddha

[325] If a man becomes fat and a great eater, if he is sleepy and rolls himself about, that fool, like a hog fed on wash, is born again and again.

It is well documented that overeating is detrimental to our health. It is equally detrimental to our spirits. When we do not exert discipline in the area of eating, we are abusing our bodies and opening ourselves up to illness and poverty. Overeating can cause us to be blind (like being asleep) to other areas of our lives that may need attention.

---

[554] Proverbs 23:1-3 (NIV).
[555] Proverbs 23:19-21 (NKJV).

Day 278

Solomon

Buddha

Give careful thought to the paths for your feet and be steadfast in all your ways.[556]

A person is praised according to their prudence, and one with a warped mind is despised.[557]

326 This mind of mine went formerly wandering about as it liked, as it listed, as it pleased; but I shall now hold it in thoroughly, as the rider who holds the hook holds in the furious elephant.

Restraining our minds, and giving careful thought to our actions, is like a rider taking the reins to hold back a furious elephant. It takes a great deal of effort and purpose. Live mindfully. Live thoughtfully. Be steadfast in this.

---

[556] Proverbs 4:26 (NIV).
[557] Proverbs 12:8 (NIV).

Day 279

Solomon

Buddha

The highway of the upright is to depart from evil; he who watches his way preserves his life.[558]

The wisdom of the prudent is to give thought to their ways, but the folly of fools is deception.[559]

[327] Be not thoughtless, watch your thoughts! Draw yourself out of the evil way, like an elephant sunk in mud.

We ought always to depart from evil, because it is like quicksand that will draw us down into it. The longer we dwell in it, the harder it is to escape. If we live mindfully, making it a habit to give thought to the actions of our daily life, we will find it easier and easier to avoid evil.

---

[558] Proverbs 16:17 (NASB).
[559] Proverbs 14:8 (NIV).

Day 280

Solomon

Perfume and incense bring joy to the heart, and the pleasantness of one's friend springs from his earnest counsel.[560]

He who walks [as a companion] with wise men is wise, but he who associates with [self-confident] fools is [a fool himself and] shall smart for it.[561]

Buddha

[328] If a man find a prudent companion who walks with him, is wise, and lives soberly, he may walk with him, overcoming all dangers, happy, but considerate.

The more we spend time with people, the more they can influence us. If we choose to spend time with foolish people, we may come to adopt their views and might be put in situations that can harm us. Finding a prudent and wise friend will help not harm us in our quest for wisdom, knowledge and the righteous life. King David wrote,

> Blessed is the man who does not walk in the counsel of the wicked or stand in the way of sinners or sit in the seat of mockers. But his delight is in the law of the LORD, and on his law he meditates day and night. He is like a tree planted by streams of water, which yields its fruit in season and whose leaf does not wither. Whatever he does prospers.[562]

---

[560] Proverbs 27:9 (NIV).
[561] Proverbs 13:20 (AMP).
[562] Psalm 1:1-3 (NIV), a psalm of King David, Solomon's father.

Day 281

Solomon	Buddha

He who walks with wise men will be wise, but the companion of fools will be destroyed.[563]

[329] If a man find no prudent companion who walks with him, is wise, and lives soberly, let him walk alone, like a king who has left his conquered country behind,— like an elephant in the forest.

[330] It is better to live alone, there is no companionship with a fool; let a man walk alone, let him commit no sin, with few wishes, like an elephant in the forest.

If the only choice of companionship is with a foolish or evil person, it is far better to be alone. A foolish companion will bring trouble with him.

---

[563] Proverbs 13:20 (NKJV).

Day 282

Solomon

Buddha

The desire of the righteous ends only in good, but the hope of the wicked only in wrath.[564]

Here is what I have seen to be good and fitting: to eat, to drink and enjoy oneself in all one's labor in which he toils under the sun during the few years of his life which God has given him; for this is his reward.[565]

The proverbs of Solomon: A wise son makes a glad father, but a foolish son is the grief of his mother.[566]

[331] If an occasion arises, friends are pleasant; enjoyment is pleasant, whatever be the cause; a good work is pleasant in the hour of death; the giving up of all grief is pleasant.

[332] Pleasant in the world is the state of a mother, pleasant the state of a father, pleasant the state of a Samana, pleasant the state of a Brahmana.

It is agreeable and enjoyable to do good and spend time with amiable people. When our children behave wisely, it makes being a mother or father very pleasant and brings us joy. Let us find satisfaction in doing good.

---

[564] Proverbs 11:23 (NIV).
[565] Ecclesiastes 5:18 (NASB).
[566] Proverbs 10:1 (NKJV).

Day 283

Solomon

For wisdom will enter your heart, and knowledge will be pleasant to your soul.[567]

Buddha

[333] Pleasant is virtue lasting to old age, pleasant is a faith firmly rooted; pleasant is attainment of intelligence, pleasant is avoiding of sins.

Virtue for a lifetime, faith firmly rooted, the attainment of intelligence, and avoiding sins, all these are pleasant. When wisdom becomes part of us, when it is stitched into our very being, knowledge is then pleasing to us.

---

[567] Proverbs 2:10 (NIV).

Chapter Twenty-Four – Thirst

(Days 284-305, Dhammapada 334-359)

This chapter focuses on desires (thirsts). If we allow our desires to run rampant, they will never be satisfied. We will always be thirsty for more. The suffering brought on by our fierce thirsts (evil desires) will fall away when we undertake to live a life of self-control.

As we dig out the root of desire, we ought to plant and foster goodness, wisdom, righteousness, and truth in our innermost being. Otherwise, we will stumble in the darkness of our passions and desires.

A foolish, out of control person is known by all. The righteous are people of integrity, walking securely, not in the recklessness of untamed desires.

Day 284

Solomon (950 BCE)

All a man's labor is for his mouth and yet the appetite is not satisfied. For what advantage does the wise man have over the fool? What advantage does the poor man have, knowing how to walk before the living? What the eyes see is better than what the soul desires. This too is futility and a striving after wind.[568]

Buddha (525 BCE)

[334] The thirst of a thoughtless man grows like a creeper; he runs from life to life, like a monkey seeking fruit in the forest.

Without self-control, our desires, our thirsts, run rampant and are never satisfied. It's like chasing after the wind. We can never catch it as it's always out of reach. We can never get our fill and are always thirsty for more.

---

[568] Ecclesiastes 6:7-9 (NASB).

Day 285

Solomon

Buddha

"Let all who are simple come to my house!" To those who have no sense she says, "Stolen water is sweet; food eaten in secret is delicious!" But little do they know that the dead are there, that her guests are deep in the realm of the dead.[569]

[335] Whomsoever this fierce thirst overcomes, full of poison, in this world, his sufferings increase like the abounding Birana grass.

The fierce thirst (desire) of a thoughtless, foolish man will overcome him and bring suffering upon him. He will be trapped by his evil, out of control desires. Righteousness and self-control will deliver the upright. Let us not be ruled by wickedness or desire.

---

[569] Proverbs 9:16-18 (NIV).

Day 286

Solomon	Buddha
No harm overtakes the righteous, but the wicked have their fill of trouble.[570]	[336] He who overcomes this fierce thirst, difficult to be conquered in this world, sufferings fall off from him, like water-drops from a lotus leaf.
. . . a wise man keeps himself under control.[571]	

The sufferings brought on by our fierce thirsts (evil desires) will fall away when we undertake to live a life of self-control. Better to be a patient and self-controlled man. King David wrote,

> *Do not be like the horse or the mule, which have no understanding but must be controlled by bit and bridle or they will not come to you.*[572]

---

[570] Proverbs 12:21 (NIV).
[571] Proverbs 29:11b (NIV).
[572] Psalm 32:9 (NIV), a psalm of King David, Solomon's father.

Day 287

Solomon	Buddha

The wicked desire the booty of evil men, but the root of the [uncompromisingly] righteous yields [richer fruitage].[573]

[337] This salutary word I tell you, 'Do ye, as many as are here assembled, dig up the root of thirst, as he who wants the sweet-scented Usira root must dig up the Birana grass, that Mara (the tempter) may not crush you again and again, as the stream crushes the reeds.'

[338] As a tree, even though it has been cut down, is firm so long as its root is safe, and grows again, thus, unless the feeders of thirst are destroyed, the pain (of life) will return again and again.

Let us dig out the root of fierce desire, so that the evil one might not crush or trample us underfoot. We ought to plant and foster goodness, wisdom, righteousness and truth in our innermost being. King David wrote,

> *Behold, You desire truth in the inner being; make me therefore to know wisdom in my inmost heart.*[574]

---

[573] Proverbs 12:12 (AMP).
[574] Psalm 51:6 (AMP), a psalm of King David, Solomon's father.

Day 288

Solomon

Buddha

But the path of the just is like the shining sun, that shines ever brighter unto the perfect day. The way of the wicked is like darkness; they do not know what makes them stumble.[575]

[339] He whose thirst running towards pleasure is exceeding strong in the thirty-six channels, the waves will carry away that misguided man, viz. his desires which are set on passion.

When our passions and desires run rampant, we don't even realize what is making us stumble in the darkness. When we live mindfully, exerting self-control and seeking wisdom and knowledge, our paths will run straight.

Day 289

Solomon

Buddha

When wisdom enters your heart, and knowledge is pleasant to your soul, discretion will preserve you; understanding will keep you, to deliver you from the way of evil.[576]

[340] The channels run everywhere, the creeper (of passion) stands sprouting; if you see the creeper springing up, cut its root by means of knowledge.

We are wise when we depart from evil desires and do not allow them to grow. Let us cut them out by the root and not leave any room for them in our lives.

---

[575] Proverbs 4:18-19 (NKJV).
[576] Proverbs 2:10-12 (NKJV).

Day 290

Solomon

A good name is better than fine perfume, and the day of death better than the day of birth. It is better to go to a house of mourning than to go to a house of feasting, for death is the destiny of every man; the living should take this to heart. Sorrow is better than laughter, because a sad face is good for the heart. The heart of the wise is in the house of mourning, but the heart of fools is in the house of pleasure.[577]

Buddha

[341] A creature's pleasures are extravagant and luxurious; sunk in lust and looking for pleasure, men undergo (again and again) birth and decay.

In between birth and death we have choices to make. We can sink into lust and pleasure, letting our passions and desires rule our lives and reaping the suffering of it, or we can choose to exert self-control and seek after wisdom and knowledge. Realizing we all will face death, it sobers us, and helps us to make lasting decisions based on wisdom and knowledge, not decisions of the moment based on desire.

---

[577] Ecclesiastes 7:1-4 (NIV).

Day 291

Solomon

Even when the fool walks along the road, his sense is lacking and he demonstrates to everyone that he is a fool.[578]

He who walks with integrity walks securely, but he who perverts his ways will become known.[579]

A scoundrel plots evil, and on their lips it is like a scorching fire.[580]

Buddha

[342] Men, driven on by thirst, run about like a snared hare; held in fetters and bonds, they undergo pain for a long time, again and again.

[343] Men, driven on by thirst, run about like a snared hare; let therefore the mendicant drive out thirst, by striving after passionlessness for himself.

As a snared hare will run about wildly seeking to escape his bonds, so a foolish man goes through life out of control and everyone can see his foolishness. We ought to be men and women of integrity, walking securely, not in the recklessness of untamed desires.

---

[578] Ecclesiastes 10:3 (NASB).
[579] Proverbs 10:9 (NKJV).
[580] Proverbs 16:27 (NIV).

Day 292

Solomon

Do not lust in your heart after her beauty or let her captivate you with her eyes, for the prostitute reduces you to a loaf of bread, and the adulteress preys upon your very life. Can a man scoop fire into his lap without his clothes being burned? Can a man walk on hot coals without his feet being scorched? So is he who sleeps with another man's wife; no one who touches her will go unpunished.[581]

Buddha

[344] He who having got rid of the forest (of lust) (i.e. after having reached Nirvana) gives himself over to forest-life (i.e. to lust), and who, when removed from the forest (i.e. from lust), runs to the forest (i.e. to lust), look at that man! though free, he runs into bondage.

Once free, why do we run back to lusts and desires that we know will harm us? It's like pouring hot coals into our laps. Will we not be burned? Let us live free from the bondage of lust.

---

[581] Proverbs 6:25-29 (NIV).

R. E. Sherman

Day 293

Solomon

A virtuous and worthy wife [earnest and strong in character] is a crowning joy to her husband, but she who makes him ashamed is as rottenness in his bones.[582]

The father of a righteous man has great joy; he who has a wise son delights in him.[583]

Buddha

[345] Wise people do not call that a strong fetter which is made of iron, wood, or hemp; far stronger is the care for precious stones and rings, for sons and a wife.

A spouse of noble character and a righteous man for a son, these are great joys, greater than that of wealth.

---

[582] Proverbs 12:4 (AMP).
[583] Proverbs 23:24 (NIV).

Day 294

Solomon

Buddha

For the living know that they will die, but the dead know nothing; they have no further reward, and even the memory of them is forgotten. Their love, their hate and their jealousy have long since vanished; never again will they have a part in anything that happens under the sun.[584]

[346] That fetter wise people call strong which drags down, yields, but is difficult to undo; after having cut this at last, people leave the world, free from cares, and leaving desires and pleasures behind.

[347] Those who are slaves to passions, run down with the stream (of desires), as a spider runs down the web which he has made himself; when they have cut this, at last, wise people leave the world free from cares, leaving all affection behind.

While we are living, we know that one day we must die. If we are wise, we know that we ought to keep a light touch while we are here, living with restraint and free from evil desires. Once we have left this world, we no longer have any worldly cares or desires. We have left everything behind.

---

[584] Ecclesiastes 9:5-6 (NIV).

Day 295

Solomon

And you mourn at last, when your flesh and your body are consumed, and say: "How I have hated instruction, and my heart despised correction! I have not obeyed the voice of my teachers, nor inclined my ear to those who instructed me! I was on the verge of total ruin, in the midst of the assembly and congregation."[585]

Buddha

[348] Give up what is before, give up what is behind, give up what is in the middle, when thou goest [sic] to the other shore of existence; if thy mind is altogether free, thou wilt not again enter into birth and decay.

Let us not wait until our last breath to discover that we have lacked discipline, wisdom and knowledge. Let us give up evil desires now, while we have time to learn, exert self-control, and live a righteous life.

---

[585] Proverbs 5:7-14 (NKJV).

Day 296

Solomon

Buddha

I denied myself nothing my eyes desired; I refused my heart no pleasure. My heart took delight in all my work, and this was the reward for all my labor. Yet when I surveyed all that my hands had done and what I had toiled to achieve, everything was meaningless, a chasing after the wind; nothing was gained under the sun.[586]

[349] If a man is tossed about by doubts, full of strong passions, and yearning only for what is delightful, his thirst will grow more and more, and he will indeed make his fetters strong.

It is our choice. Will we be ruled by our desires, seeking those things we find pleasurable in this life, or will we take delight in wisdom? When he was young, Solomon sought wisdom above all else. Sadly, as Solomon grew older, he hoarded women, gold and horses, all of which the Torah prohibited. Consequently, later in his life, God withdrew his blessings from Solomon.[587]

---

[586] Ecclesiastes 2:10-11 (NIV).
[587] 1 Kings 3:5-12, Deuteronomy 17:14-17, 1 Kings 11:1-13. Moses lived at least 200 years prior to Solomon.

Day 297

Solomon

Do not be wise in your own eyes; fear the LORD and depart from evil. It will be health to your flesh, and strength to your bones.[588]

The fear of the LORD leads to life: then one rests content, untouched by trouble.[589]

Buddha

[350] If a man delights in quieting doubts, and, always reflecting, dwells on what is not delightful (the impurity of the body, &c. [sic]), he certainly will remove, nay, he will cut the fetter of Mara.

[351] He who has reached the consummation, who does not tremble, who is without thirst and without sin, he has broken all the thorns of life: this will be his last body.

Let us not be wise in our own eyes (prideful), but be quiet, mindful and meditative. Let us actively cut the bonds of evil in our lives. Doing so will result in good health, physically and mentally.

---

[588] Proverbs 3:7-8 (NKJV).
[589] Proverbs 19:23 (NIV).

Day 298

Solomon

Buddha

Wise people store up knowledge, but the mouth of the foolish is near destruction.[590]

The simple acquire folly, but the prudent are crowned with knowledge.[591]

Gold there is, and rubies in abundance, but lips that speak knowledge are a rare jewel.[592]

[352] He who is without thirst and without affection, who understands the words and their interpretation, who knows the order of letters (those which are before and which are after), he has received his last body, he is called the great sage, the great man.

One who lips speak knowledge, who is not ruled by desire, and who understands the law, this is a great sage, a wise man. We ought to store up knowledge and live prudently, then we too shall be wise.

---

[590] Proverbs 10:14 (NKJV).
[591] Proverbs 14:18 (AMP).
[592] Proverbs 20:15 (NIV).

Day 299

Solomon

So I became great and excelled more than all who were before me in Jerusalem. Also my wisdom remained with me.[593]

Every way of a man is right in his own eyes, but the Lord weighs the hearts.[594]

Buddha

[353] 'I have conquered all, I know all, in all conditions of life I am free from taint; I have left all, and through the destruction of thirst I am free; having learnt myself, whom shall I teach?'

Then I looked on all the works that my hands had done and on the labor in which I had toiled; and indeed all was vanity and grasping for the wind. There was no profit under the sun. Then I turned myself to consider wisdom and madness and folly; for what can the man do who succeeds the king?— Only what he has already done. Then I saw that wisdom excels folly as light excels darkness.[595]

Once we think we are free from all evil and are completely self-controlled, let us not substitute pride for desire. It is a daily choice to continue in humility and restraint.

---

[593] Ecclesiastes 2:9 (NKJV).
[594] Proverbs 21:2 (NKJV).
[595] Ecclesiastes 2:11-13 (NKJV).

Day 300

Solomon	Buddha

I long for your salvation, O LORD, and your law is my delight.[596]

If your law had not been my delight, I would have perished in my affliction.[597]

[354] The gift of the law exceeds all gifts; the sweetness of the law exceeds all sweetness; the delight in the law exceeds all delights; the extinction of thirst overcomes all pain.

The gift and the sweetness of the law, let us savor that truth. Night and day, let the law be our delight. Without it we would be lost, subject to our evil desires, and suffering pain, distress, misery and physical affliction.

---

[596] Psalm 119:174 (NIV).
[597] Psalm 119:92 (NASB).

Day 301

Solomon

The wise woman builds her house, but the foolish pulls it down with her hands.[598]

In the house of the wise are stores of choice food and oil, but a foolish man devours all he has.[599]

Buddha

[355] Pleasures destroy the foolish, if they look not for the other shore; the foolish by his thirst for pleasures destroys himself, as if he were his own enemy.

By our foolishness and evil desires we destroy our own lives, our own homes, our own families. Rather than living for momentary desires, we ought to mindfully do good, and seek wisdom and knowledge, knowing that these will keep destruction at bay.

---

[598] Proverbs 14:1 (NKJV).
[599] Proverbs 21:20 (NIV).

Day 302

Solomon	Buddha
The righteousness of the upright [their rectitude in every area and relation] shall deliver them, but the treacherous shall be taken in their own iniquity and greedy desire.[600]	[356] The fields are damaged by weeds, mankind is damaged by passion: therefore a gift bestowed on the passionless brings great reward.
The desire of the righteous ends only in good, but the hope of the wicked only in wrath.[601]	

Like weeds choking out an excellent crop, so our passions and evil desires can damage and destroy our lives and the lives of those around us. Let us not be trapped by our evil desires, but be freed from their influence and destructive nature.

---

[600] Proverbs 11:6 (AMP).
[601] Proverbs 11:23 (NIV).

Day 303

Solomon

Buddha

Hatred stirs up strife, but love covers all sins.[602]

Let not mercy and kindness [shutting out all hatred and selfishness] and truth [shutting out all deliberate hypocrisy or falsehood] forsake you; bind them about your neck, write them upon the tablet of your heart.[603]

[357] The fields are damaged by weeds, mankind is damaged by hatred: therefore a gift bestowed on those who do not hate brings great reward.

Hatred is a destructive force. It stirs up all sorts of conflicts and problems in our lives. Let us fill our hearts with love, mercy and kindness, which dissipates hatred and covers over errors and sins.

---

[602] Proverbs 10:12 (NKJV).
[603] Proverbs 3:3 (AMP).

Day 304

Solomon

Buddha

When pride comes, then comes disgrace, but with humility comes wisdom.[604]

Pride goes before destruction, and a haughty spirit before a fall.[605]

[358] The fields are damaged by weeds, mankind is damaged by vanity: therefore a gift bestowed on those who are free from vanity brings great reward.

Being vain about one's appearance, abilities, or having no other purpose in life than selfish pride is damaging to ourselves and those around us. There is no room for the spiritual life in someone who is vain and prideful. King David wrote,

In his pride the wicked does not seek him; in all his thoughts there is no room for God.[606]

---

[604] Proverbs 11:2 (NIV).
[605] Proverbs 16:18 (NKJV).
[606] Psalm 10:4 (NIV), a psalm of King David, Solomon's father.

Day 305

Solomon

Do not desire her beauty in your heart, nor let her capture you with her eyelids. For on account of a harlot one is reduced to a loaf of bread, and an adulteress hunts for the precious life. Can a man take fire in his bosom and his clothes not be burned? Or can a man walk on hot coals and his feet not be scorched?[607]

The righteousness of the upright delivers them, but the unfaithful are trapped by evil desires.[608]

Buddha

[359] The fields are damaged by weeds, mankind is damaged by lust: therefore a gift bestowed on those who are free from lust brings great reward.

Just as passion (evil desires), hatred, and vanity (pride) damage our lives, so does lust. Lust can consume us, devastate our lives, destroy our families, ruin us financially, and even cost lives. Our culture might try to convince us that we can "get away with it," but the truth is much darker and more devastating. Let us experience freedom from lust so that we may flourish and grow spiritually.

---

[607] Proverbs 6:25-28 (NASB).
[608] Proverbs 11:6 (NIV).

Chapter Twenty-Five –

The Bhikshu (Mendicant)

(Days 306-325, Dhammapada 360-381)

A mendicant is a monk (beggar) who relies on charity to survive. This chapter addresses the conduct and life of a mendicant. Restraint and self-control in all aspects of life are encouraged.

Some of the instructions include delighting in and meditating on the law, speaking wisely and calmly, not despising what he has received, being free from pride, acting with kindness, being emptied of passion and desire and being tranquil.

Day 306

Solomon (950 BCE)

He who loves purity of heart and has grace on his lips, the king will be his friend.[609]

A [self-confident] fool utters all his anger, but a wise man holds it back and stills it.[610]

Like a city that is broken into and without walls is a man who has no control over his spirit.[611]

Buddha (525 BCE)

[360] Restraint in the eye is good, good is restraint in the ear, in the nose restraint is good, good is restraint in the tongue.

[361] In the body restraint is good, good is restraint in speech, in thought restraint is good, good is restraint in all things. A Bhikshu, restrained in all things, is freed from all pain.

Having restraint over our bodies, what we see and hear, and exerting self-control when we speak is essential to fostering a spiritual life. A foolish person utters every thought and gives voice to every emotion with no regard for self-control. Keeping a pure heart and grace on our lips is wise.

---

[609] Proverbs 22:11 (NKJV).
[610] Proverbs 29:11 (AMP).
[611] Proverbs 25:28 (NASB).

Day 307

Solomon

Buddha

Above all else, keep your heart with all diligence, for out of it spring the issues of life. Put away from you a deceitful mouth, and put perverse lips far from you. Let your eyes look straight ahead, and your eyelids look right before you. Ponder the path of your feet, and let all your ways be established. Do not turn to the right or the left; remove your foot from evil.[612]

362 He who controls his hand, he who controls his feet, he who controls his speech, he who is well controlled, he who delights inwardly, who is collected, who is solitary and content, him they call Bhikshu.

Having self-control might seem like a nebulous statement, but when we start to look at the very practical ways we can carry that out in our lives, it becomes very doable. Put away deceit. Don't have wandering eyes (coveting what others have). Consider our daily path through life. Keep from doing evil. Choose to do good. Be content. These are a few of the very practical things we can do every day to exercise self-control.

---

[612] Proverbs 4:23-27 (NKJV).

Day 308

Solomon	Buddha
He who covers over an offense promotes love, but whoever repeats the matter separates close friends.[613] Pleasant words are like a honeycomb, sweetness to the soul and health to the bones.[614] The tongue of the righteous is choice silver, but the heart of the wicked is of little value.[615]	[363] The Bhikshu who controls his mouth, who speaks wisely and calmly, who teaches the meaning and the law, his word is sweet.

Self-control over our mouths involves speaking wisely and calmly, promoting love, not repeating offenses or speaking badly of others, and teaching the law and its meaning. When we speak the truth and speak pleasantly, it is sweetness to our souls and health to our bodies.

---

[613] Proverbs 17:9 (NIV).
[614] Proverbs 16:24 (NKJV).
[615] Proverbs 10:20 (NIV).

Day 309

Solomon

How can a young man cleanse his way? By taking heed according to Your word. With my whole heart I have sought You; Oh, let me not wander from Your commandments! Your word I have hidden in my heart, that I might not sin against You. . . . I have rejoiced in the way of Your testimonies, as much as in all riches. I will meditate on Your precepts, and contemplate Your ways. I will delight myself in Your statutes; I will not forget Your word.[616]

Buddha

[364] He who dwells in the law, delights in the law, meditates on the law, follows the law, that Bhikshu will never fall away from the true law.

Take heed of and dwell in the law, delight in the law, meditate and contemplate on the law, seek after and follow the law . . . in doing all this, we will neither forget the law nor will we wander or fall away from it.

---

[616] Psalm 119:9-16 (NKJV).

Day 310

Solomon

Buddha

A heart at peace gives life to the body, but envy rots the bones.[617]

And I saw that all labor and all achievement spring from man's envy of his neighbor. This too is meaningless, a chasing after the wind.[618]

[365] Let him not despise what he has received, nor ever envy others: a mendicant who envies others does not obtain peace of mind.

We can spend our entire life trying to keep up with our neighbors. We can put ourselves in financial distress trying to own all the same things or better, more expensive ones. We can allow envy to literally consume our bodies (rot our bones). We can compete until we drop dead, but what does that accomplish? Better to be content and have peace of mind than to envy others and end up sick and poor.

---

[617] Proverbs 14:30 (NIV).
[618] Ecclesiastes 4:4 (NIV).

Day 311

Solomon

Buddha

Better is an handful with quietness, than both the hands full with travail and vexation of spirit.[619]

[366] A Bhikshu who, though he receives little, does not despise what he has received, even the gods will praise him, if his life is pure, and if he is not slothful.

We are better off to be content and grateful with less than to strive and toil for more and have no peace or tranquility. This does not mean to be slothful, but simply not to strive for more just for the sake of having more.

Day 312

Solomon

Buddha

When pride comes, then comes shame; but with the humble is wisdom.[620]

A man's pride will bring him low, but a humble spirit will obtain honor.[621]

[367] He who never identifies himself with name and form, and does not grieve over what is no more, he indeed is called a Bhikshu.

When we are concerned with outward appearances, our pride takes over. Better to have a humble spirit than to be proud and puffed up over possessions and prestige.

---

[619] Ecclesiastes 4:6 (KJV).
[620] Proverbs 11:2 (NKJV).
[621] Proverbs 29:23 (NASB).

Day 313

Solomon

The merciful, kind, and generous man benefits himself [for his deeds return to bless him], but he who is cruel and callous [to the wants of others] brings on himself retribution.[622]

He who despises his neighbor sins [against God, his fellowman, and himself], but happy (blessed and fortunate) is he who is kind and merciful to the poor.[623]

Buddha

[368] The Bhikshu who acts with kindness, who is calm in the doctrine of Buddha, will reach the quiet place (Nirvana), cessation of natural desires, and happiness.

Kindness is an important trait to cultivate in our spiritual lives. As well as helping others, thinking of them, doing kind acts, and having compassion are ways to combat envy and pride. When we are kind to others, we reap a reward of blessing upon ourselves as well.

---

[622] Proverbs 11:17 (AMP).
[623] Proverbs 14:21 (AMP).

Day 314

Solomon

Buddha

Hatred stirs up contentions, but love covers all transgressions.[624]

Do not let kindness and truth leave you; bind them around your neck, write them on the tablet of your heart.[625]

[369] O Bhikshu, empty this boat! if emptied, it will go quickly; having cut off passion and hatred thou wilt go to Nirvana.

We can travel through life better without evil desires and hatred, like a boat freely skimming through the water. Better to let love be ever present in our hearts.

---

[624] Proverbs 10:12 (AMP).
[625] Proverbs 3:3 (NASB).

Day 315

Solomon	Buddha
Above all else, guard your heart, for it is the wellspring of life. Put away perversity from your mouth; keep corrupt talk far from your lips. Let your eyes look straight ahead, fix your gaze directly before you. Make level paths for your feet and take only ways that are firm. Do not swerve to the right or the left; keep your foot from evil.[626]	[370] Cut off the five (senses), leave the five, rise above the five. A Bhikshu, who has escaped from the five fetters, he is called Oghatinna, 'saved from the flood.'

Our five senses, the ability to see, hear, smell, taste and touch, left unchecked can lead us into evil desires. They can become an insatiable force in our lives. We ought to guard ourselves from unchecked desires, and exert self-control in these five areas.

---

[626] Proverbs 4:23-27 (NIV).

Day 316

Solomon

Buddha

Say to wisdom, "You are my sister," and call understanding your kinsman; they will keep you from the adulteress, from the wayward wife with her seductive words. . . . Do not let your heart turn to her ways or stray into her paths. Many are the victims she has brought down; her slain are a mighty throng. Her house is a highway to the grave, leading down to the chambers of death.[627]

371 Meditate, O Bhikshu, and be not heedless! Do not direct thy thought to what gives pleasure that thou mayest not for thy heedlessness have to swallow the iron ball (in hell), and that thou mayest not cry out when burning, 'This is pain.'

Reckless pursuit of pleasure leads to death. It kills our spirits and may kill our bodies too. We ought to be mindful to restrain ourselves from such pleasure seeking.

---

[627] Proverbs 7:4–5, 25–27 (NIV).

Day 317

Solomon

To know wisdom and instruction, to discern the sayings of understanding, to receive instruction in wise behavior, righteousness, justice and equity; to give prudence to the naive, to the youth knowledge and discretion, a wise man will hear and increase in learning, and a man of understanding will acquire wise counsel, to understand a proverb and a figure, the words of the wise and their riddles.[628]

Buddha

[372] Without knowledge there is no meditation, without meditation there is no knowledge: he who has knowledge and meditation is near unto Nirvana.

[373] A Bhikshu who has entered his empty house, and whose mind is tranquil, feels a more than human delight when he sees the law clearly.

Seeking after wisdom and knowledge combined with contemplation and meditation is the perfect combination for the serious student of spiritual matters.

---

[628] Proverbs 1:2-6 (NASB).

Day 318

Solomon

My son, if you accept my words and store up my commands within you, turning your ear to wisdom and applying your heart to understanding, and if you call out for insight and cry aloud for understanding, and if you look for it as for silver and search for it as for hidden treasure. . . . Then you will understand what is right and just and fair—every good path. For wisdom will enter your heart, and knowledge will be pleasant to your soul. Discretion will protect you, and understanding will guard you.[629]

Buddha

[374] As soon as he has considered the origin and destruction of the elements (khandha) of the body, he finds happiness and joy which belong to those who know the immortal (Nirvana).

Exerting self-control over our bodies and seeking earnestly after wisdom and knowledge, this is the wise path where we find joy and happiness.

---

[629] Proverbs 2:1-4, 9-11 (NIV).

Day 319

Solomon

The righteous should choose his friends carefully, for the way of the wicked leads them astray.[630]

Make no friendships with a man given to anger, and with a wrathful man do not associate.[631]

Buddha

[375] And this is the beginning here for a wise Bhikshu: watchfulness over the senses, contentedness, restraint under the law; keep noble friends whose life is pure, and who are not slothful.

Our choice in friends can have a significant impact on our lives. If we choose wisely, they will influence us for good. If we choose recklessly, they may bring harm upon us, even to the point of putting our lives in jeopardy.

---

[630] Proverbs 12:26 (NKJV).
[631] Proverbs 22:24 (AMP).

Day 320

Solomon

A generous man will prosper; he who refreshes others will himself be refreshed.[632]

He who has a generous eye will be blessed, for he gives of his bread to the poor.[633]

Buddha

[376] Let him live in charity, let him be perfect in his duties; then in the fulness [sic] of delight he will make an end of suffering.

Generosity (in spirit, in giving, in compassion and love) is a hallmark of a righteous life and will not only result in doing good to others, but result in being refreshed ourselves.

Day 321

Solomon

Better a meal of vegetables where there is love than a fattened calf with hatred.[634]

Buddha

[377] As the Vassika plant sheds its withered flowers, men should shed passion and hatred, O ye Bhikshus!

Shed passion (evil desires) and hatred. Better to have nothing but a bowl of vegetables where there is love than to be showered with worldly possessions where there is hate.

---

[632] Proverbs 11:25 (NIV).
[633] Proverbs 22:9 (NKJV).
[634] Proverbs 15:17 (NIV).

Day 322

Solomon

Buddha

The words of wise men
heard in quiet are better
than the shouts of him who
rules among fools.[635]

A gentle answer turns away
wrath, but a harsh word stirs
up anger.[636]

[378] The Bhikshu whose body
and tongue and mind are
quieted, who is collected,
and has rejected the baits of
the world, he is called quiet.

As we collect our thoughts and quiet our bodies and tongues, we find that a gentle reply can dissipate anger in others, and that others will listen more intently to us than if we were out of control and shouting. There is power in a wise word spoken gently.

---

[635] Ecclesiastes 9:17 (AMP).
[636] Proverbs 15:1 (NIV).

Day 323

Solomon

The wisdom of the prudent is to give thought to their ways, but the folly of fools is deception.[637]

A simple man believes anything, but a prudent man gives thought to his steps.[638]

Buddha

[379] Rouse thyself by thyself, examine thyself by thyself, thus self-protected and attentive wilt thou live happily, O Bhikshu!

Giving thought to our ways, or examining ourselves and making course corrections in our lives is of great value and should not be underrated. Socrates echoed the sentiment when he wrote, "The unexamined life is not worth living."[639] Jesus taught that a lack of self-examination can lead to hypocrisy.

> Why do you look at the speck of sawdust in your brother's eye and pay no attention to the plank in your own eye? How can you say to your brother, "Let me take the speck out of your eye," when all the time there is a plank in your own eye? You hypocrite, first take the plank out of your own eye, and then you will see clearly to remove the speck from your brother's eye.[640]

---

[637] Proverbs 14:8 (NIV).
[638] Proverbs 14:15 (NIV).
[639] Socrates lived from 469 BCE to 399 BCE.
[640] Matthew 7:3-5 (NIV).

Day 324

Solomon	Buddha

When swelling and pride come, then emptiness and shame come also, but with the humble (those who are lowly, who have been pruned or chiseled by trial, and renounce self) are skillful and godly Wisdom and soundness.[641]

380 For self is the lord of self, self is the refuge of self; therefore curb thyself as the merchant curbs a good horse.

Like we would guide a willing horse or mule, we ought to control ourselves, making constant, slight corrections as we walk through life. King David wrote,

Do not be like the horse or the mule, which have no understanding but must be controlled by bit and bridle or they will not come to you. [642]

---

[641] Proverbs 11:2 (AMP).
[642] Psalm 32:9 (NIV), a psalm of King David, Solomon's father.

Day 325

Solomon

Buddha

My son, if you receive my words, and treasure my commands within you, so that you incline your ear to wisdom, and apply your heart to understanding; yes, if you cry out for discernment, and lift up your voice for understanding, if you seek her as silver, and search for her as for hidden treasures; . . . Then you will understand righteousness and justice, equity and every good path. When wisdom enters your heart, and knowledge is pleasant to your soul, discretion will preserve you; understanding will keep you.[643]

[381] The Bhikshu, full of delight, who is calm in the doctrine of Buddha will reach the quiet place (Nirvana), cessation of natural desires, and happiness.

When we seek wisdom and knowledge, and pursue it earnestly, it becomes part of us. It becomes our delight and is pleasant to our souls. We can rest in the knowledge that it protects and guards us.

---

[643] Proverbs 2:1-4, 9-11 (NKJV).

Chapter Twenty-Six –

The Brahmana (Arhat)

(Days 326-365, Dhammapada 383-423)

An *arhat* is "the worthy one" or "the one who has destroyed the foes of afflictions."[644] This lengthy chapter covers the attributes of an *arhat*.

For example, he is fearless and unshackled, thoughtful, blameless, settled, dutiful, and without passions. He is rid of evil and walks quietly. He is free from anger and does not attack another, even someone aggressive towards him. He does not offend by body, word, or thought, and he possesses wisdom and knowledge.

---

[644] "Arhat," Wikipedia.org, http://en.wikipedia.org/wiki/Arhat, retrieved October 29, 2013.

Day 326

Solomon (950 BCE)

Do not enter the path of the wicked, and do not walk in the way of evil. Avoid it, do not travel on it; turn away from it and pass on. For they do not sleep unless they have done evil; and their sleep is taken away unless they make someone fall. For they eat the bread of wickedness, and drink the wine of violence.[645]

Buddha (525 BCE)

[383] Stop the stream valiantly, drive away the desires, O Brahmana! When you have understood the destruction of all that was made, you will understand that which was not made.

We have a choice to make. Solomon likens it to choosing whether to walk on a path or not. Buddha likens it to a stream, which needs to be stopped. Either way, we must choose whether to indulge evil desires or drive them away.

---

[645] Proverbs 4:14-17 (NKJV).

Day 327

Solomon

Buddha

Receive my instruction in preference to [striving for] silver, and knowledge rather than choice gold, for skillful and godly Wisdom is better than rubies or pearls, and all the things that may be desired are not to be compared to it.[646]

384 If the Brahmana has reached the other shore in both laws (in restraint and contemplation), all bonds vanish from him who has obtained knowledge.

Obtaining wisdom and knowledge is finer and more important than having all the wealth that can be imagined. The fruit of wisdom and knowledge in our lives is that we can exercise restraint, spend time in meditation, and are free from the bonds of evil desires.

---

[646] Proverbs 8:10-11 (AMP).

Day 328

Solomon

Buddha

My son, let them not escape from your sight, but keep sound and godly Wisdom and discretion, and they will be life to your inner self, and a gracious ornament to your neck (your outer self). Then you will walk in your way securely and in confident trust, and you shall not dash your foot or stumble. When you lie down, you shall not be afraid; yes, you shall lie down, and your sleep shall be sweet. Be not afraid of sudden terror and panic, nor of the stormy blast or the storm and ruin of the wicked when it comes [for you will be guiltless], for the Lord shall be your confidence, firm and strong, and shall keep your foot from being caught [in a trap or some hidden danger].[647]

[385] He for whom there is neither this nor that shore, nor both, him, the fearless and unshackled, I call indeed a Brahmana.

To be fearless and unshackled by evil desires, this is accomplished through keeping wisdom before us. Meditating on it day and night, it will become part of us, ever present in times of difficulty and decision-making. Wisdom will keep us from becoming trapped by hidden dangers, because we will already be walking on the wise and righteous path.

---

[647] Proverbs 3:21-26 (AMP).

Day 329

Solomon

For the LORD gives wisdom, and from his mouth come knowledge and understanding. He holds victory in store for the upright, he is a shield to those whose walk is blameless, for he guards the course of the just and protects the way of his faithful ones.[648]

Buddha

386 He who is thoughtful, blameless, settled, dutiful, without passions, and who has attained the highest end, him I call indeed a Brahmana.

We ought to strive to be blameless, thoughtful, dutiful, and without evil desires. Faithful in our habits of meditation and study (seeking wisdom and knowledge), we know we are secure and guarded by this wise path. In Psalms we read,

> LORD, who may dwell in your sanctuary? Who may live on your holy hill? He whose walk is blameless and who does what is righteous, who speaks the truth from his heart.[649] For the LORD God is a sun and shield; the LORD bestows favor and honor; no good thing does he withhold from those whose walk is blameless.[650]

---

[648] Proverbs 2:6-8 (NIV).
[649] Psalm 15:1-2 (NIV), a psalm of King David, Solomon's father.
[650] Psalm 84:11 (NIV).

Day 330

Solomon	Buddha
The path of the righteous is like the morning sun, shining ever brighter till the full light of day.[651]	[387] The sun is bright by day, the moon shines by night, the warrior is bright in his armour [sic], the Brahmana is bright in his meditation; but Buddha, the Awakened, is bright with splendour [sic] day and night.

The law is a lamp to our feet and a light for our path. It is as bright as the sun. Let us love it and meditate on it day and night. Let it be sweetness to us, like honey to our mouths.

---

[651] Proverbs 4:18 (NIV).

Day 331

Solomon

A wise man fears and departs from evil, but a fool rages and is self-confident.[652]

The highway of the upright is to depart from evil; he who keeps his way preserves his soul.[653]

Buddha

[388] Because a man is rid of evil, therefore he is called Brahmana; because he walks quietly, therefore he is called Samana; because he has sent away his own impurities, therefore he is called Pravragita (Pabbagita, a pilgrim).

We ought to be rid of evil, depart from it, send away impurities, and seek the quiet, meditative life that guards us from evil. Let us walk on the highway of the righteous and upright, and thereby preserve our souls and lives.

---

[652] Proverbs 14:16 (NKJV).
[653] Proverbs 16:17 (NKJV).

Day 332

Solomon	Buddha

Do not associate with a man given to anger; or go with a hot-tempered man, or you will learn his ways and find a snare for yourself.[654]

Those who guard their mouths and their tongues keep themselves from calamity.[655]

[389] No one should attack a Brahmana, but no Brahmana (if attacked) should let himself fly at his aggressor! Woe to him who strikes a Brahmana, more woe to him who flies at his aggressor!

We ought to put aside anger and physical abuse, and we ought not to associate people who are given to rage and violence, or we might become ensnared in such behavior. Let us restrain any impulse to anger and violence.

---

[654] Proverbs 22:24-25 (NASB).
[655] Proverbs 21:23 (NIV).

Day 333

Solomon

Buddha

A wise man fears the LORD and shuns evil, but a fool is hotheaded and reckless. A quick-tempered man does foolish things, and a crafty man is hated.[656]

[390] It advantages a Brahmana not a little if he holds his mind back from the pleasures of life; when all wish to injure has vanished, pain will cease.

In our anger, we might do many things we would regret if we had a cooler head at the moment. The injury caused can be very hard or even impossible to repair. Better to remain calm and thoughtful than to have regrets over harsh, reckless words.

Day 334

Solomon

Buddha

. . . a wise man keeps himself under control.[657]

[391] Him I call indeed a Brahmana who does not offend by body, word, or thought, and is controlled on these three points.

A wise, righteous man keeps himself under control, controlling his body, actions, speech, and thoughts. Let us rein ourselves in, and consider the virtues of restraint.

---

[656] Proverbs 14:16-17 (NIV).
[657] Proverbs 29:11b (NIV).

Day 335

Solomon

Your testimonies are wonderful; therefore my soul observes them. The unfolding of Your words gives light; it gives understanding to the simple. I opened my mouth wide and panted, for I longed for Your commandments.[658]

Buddha

[392] After a man has once understood the law as taught by the Well-awakened (Buddha), let him worship it carefully, as the Brahmana worships the sacrificial fire.

When we understand the law and the light and life it brings into our lives, the result is that we long for it, we pant after it, we adore it. Let us meditate on and observe the law and let it work wonders in our lives.

---

[658] Psalm 119:129-131 (NASB).

Day 336

Solomon

LORD, who may dwell in your sanctuary? Who may live on your holy hill? He whose walk is blameless and who does what is righteous, who speaks the truth from his heart.[659]

Buddha

[393] A man does not become a Brahmana by his platted hair, by his family, or by birth; in whom there is truth and righteousness, he is blessed, he is a Brahmana.

As human beings, we often make judgments based on the external appearance of people, but we need to remember that it is not our outward appearance that makes us righteous. It is not because we wear a certain piece of clothing or cut our hair a certain way. It is not because of our family or any sort of rank or prestige in this life. In the First Book of Samuel, God was giving direction to Samuel regarding the choice of a King over Israel.

But the LORD said to Samuel, "Do not look at his appearance or at his physical stature, because I have refused him. For the LORD does not see as man sees; for man looks at the outward appearance, but the LORD looks at the heart."[660]

---

[659] Psalm 15:1-2 (NIV), a psalm of King David, Solomon's father.
[660] 1 Samuel 16:7 (NKJV).

Day 337

Solomon

Buddha

The lamp of the LORD searches the spirit of a man; it searches out his inmost being.[661]

[394] What is the use of platted hair, O fool! what of the raiment of goat-skins? Within thee there is ravening, but the outside thou makest clean.

Imagine biting into a shiny red apple only to discover that the inside is worm-eaten. Of what use is that tempting exterior, if the interior is rotten and not worth eating. We can pretend all we like, but the purity of a righteous life must begin with the lamp of the law searching out the darkest places in our minds and hearts and purifying them. King David wrote, "Behold, You desire truth in the innermost being, and in the hidden part You will make me know wisdom."[662]

---

[661] Proverbs 20:27 (NIV).
[662] Psalm 51:6 (NASB), a psalm of King David, Solomon's father.

Day 338

Solomon

Buddha

I cry out with my whole heart; hear me, O LORD! I will keep Your statutes. I cry out to You; save me, and I will keep Your testimonies. I rise before the dawning of the morning, and cry for help; I hope in Your word. My eyes are awake through the night watches, that I may meditate on Your word.[663]

395 The man who wears dirty raiments [*sic*], who is emaciated and covered with veins, who lives alone in the forest, and meditates, him I call indeed a Brahmana.

Whether we live alone in a forest, or in the middle of a large family in a big city, meditation is integral to the righteous life. Let us meditate on the law and let it work its wisdom in our lives.

---

[663] Psalm 119:145-148 (NKJV).

Day 339

Solomon   **Buddha**

Better is the poor who walks in his integrity than one perverse in his ways, though he be rich.[664]

[396] I do not call a man a Brahmana because of his origin or of his mother. He is indeed arrogant, and he is wealthy: but the poor, who is free from all attachments, him I call indeed a Brahmana.

Better to be poor and blameless than to be rich and arrogant and burdened with evil desires.

Day 340

Solomon   **Buddha**

For the backsliding of the simple shall slay them, and the careless ease of [self-confident] fools shall destroy them. But whoso hearkens to me [Wisdom] shall dwell securely and in confident trust and shall be quiet, without fear or dread of evil.[665]

[397] Him I call indeed a Brahmana who has cut all fetters, who never trembles, is independent and unshackled.

Foolish ways will bring harm upon us. Better to cut out evil from our lives. When we live a righteous life, we can be at peace and free from fear and trembling.

---

[664] Proverbs 28:6 (NKJV).
[665] Proverbs 1:32-33 (AMP).

Day 341

Solomon

Buddha

Be sure of this: The wicked will not go unpunished, but those who are righteous will go free.[666]

[398] Him I call indeed a Brahmana who has cut the strap and the thong, the chain with all that pertains to it, who has burst the bar, and is awakened.

We can choose to be shackled to evil, or we can choose a righteous, wise path. The consequences of evil conduct brings punishment, but the wise, righteous path secures blessing and freedom.

---

[666] Proverbs 11:21 (NIV).

Day 342

Solomon	Buddha
The LORD is my light and my salvation; whom shall I fear? The LORD is the strength of my life; of whom shall I be afraid? When the wicked came against me to eat up my flesh, my enemies and foes, they stumbled and fell. Though an army may encamp against me, my heart shall not fear; though war may rise against me, in this I will be confident.[667]	[399] Him I call indeed a Brahmana who, though he has committed no offence [*sic*], endures reproach, bonds, and stripes, who has endurance for his force, and strength for his army.

When the righteous man is punished, even though he does not deserve it, he can endure it with a quiet strength.

---

[667] Psalm 27:1-3 (NKJV), a psalm of King David, Solomon's father.

Day 343

Solomon

Mockers stir up a city, but wise men turn away anger.[668]

A fool gives full vent to his anger, but a wise man keeps himself under control.[669]

Buddha

[400] Him I call indeed a Brahmana who is free from anger, dutiful, virtuous, without appetite, who is subdued, and has received his last body.

A fool can stir up an entire city with his anger, but a wise man is one who controls his emotions, appetites, and behaviors. Let us choose to be wise and exert self-control.

---

[668] Proverbs 29:8 (NIV).
[669] Proverbs 29:11 (NIV).

Day 344

Solomon

A fool finds pleasure in evil conduct, but a man of understanding delights in wisdom.[670]

The righteousness of the upright will deliver them, but the unfaithful will be caught by their lust.[671]

Buddha

[401] Him I call indeed a Brahmana who does not cling to pleasures, like water on a lotus leaf, like a mustard seed on the point of a needle.

If we find pleasure in doing evil, we are foolish. Let us not cling to evil like a pleasure, but take delight in wisdom. Otherwise, our evil desires will trap us.

Day 345

Solomon

If you are wise, your wisdom will reward you; if you are a mocker, you alone will suffer.[672]

Buddha

[402] Him I call indeed a Brahmana who, even here, knows the end of his suffering, has put down his burden, and is unshackled.

A simple, foolish man keeps doing the wrong he is doing in spite of suffering for it. A wise man sees the error of his ways and decides to stop doing evil.

---

[670] Proverbs 10:23 (NIV).
[671] Proverbs 11:6 (NKJV).
[672] Proverbs 9:12 (NIV).

Day 346

Solomon

A prudent man sees the evil and hides himself, but the simple pass on and are punished [with suffering].[673]

Buddha

[403] Him I call indeed a Brahmana whose knowledge is deep, who possesses wisdom, who knows the right way and the wrong, and has attained the highest end.

A wise man possesses knowledge and understanding. He knows the difference between the right and wrong path. He sees evil and departs from it. The foolish just continue on and suffer.

Day 347

Solomon

Seldom set foot in your neighbor's house, lest he become weary of you and hate you.[674]

Whoever has no rule over his own spirit is like a city broken down, without walls.[675]

Buddha

[404] Him I call indeed a Brahmana who keeps aloof both from laymen and from mendicants, who frequents no houses, and has but few desires.

It's not wise to wear out your welcome by visiting others too often. Balancing time alone for study and meditation, and time with others, as we perform acts of kindness, is another aspect of self-control.

---

[673] Proverbs 22:3 (AMP).
[674] Proverbs 25:17 (NKJV).
[675] Proverbs 25:28 (NKJV).

Day 348

Solomon	Buddha
Do not say, "I will repay evil"; wait for the LORD, and He will save you.[676]	[405] Him I call indeed a Brahmana who finds no fault with other beings, whether feeble or strong, and does not kill nor cause slaughter.
Bloodthirsty men hate a man of integrity and seek to kill the upright.[677]	

Faultfinding and judging can escalate into hatred and murder. We ought not to pay back wrongs done to us or harbor hatred in our hearts.

Day 349

Solomon	Buddha
A soft answer turns away wrath, but a harsh word stirs up anger.[678]	[406] Him I call indeed a Brahmana who is tolerant with the intolerant, mild with fault-finders, and free from passion among the passionate.
Hatred stirs up dissension, but love covers over all wrongs.[679]	

It is often disarming to people when we do not respond in kind. For the angry person, a soft or gentle reply can often diffuse their anger. For a judgmental person, a kind word might silence them. Let us behave in a humble, loving way, free from evil passions.

---

[676] Proverbs 20:22 (NASB).
[677] Proverbs 29:10 (NIV).
[678] Proverbs 15:1 (NKJV).
[679] Proverbs 10:12 (NIV).

Day 350

Solomon

Buddha

Hatred stirs up strife, but love covers all sins.[680]

Pride goes before destruction, and a haughty spirit before stumbling.[681]

A heart at peace gives life to the body, but envy rots the bones.[682]

[407] Him I call indeed a Brahmana from whom anger and hatred, pride and envy have dropt like a mustard seed from the point of a needle.

As a mustard seed will not adhere to the point of a needle, so we ought to let anger, hatred, pride and envy drop away from us.

Day 351

Solomon

Buddha

A wise man's heart guides his mouth, and his lips promote instruction. Pleasant words are a honeycomb, sweet to the soul and healing to the bones.[683]

[408] Him I call indeed a Brahmana who utters true speech, instructive and free from harshness, so that he offend[s] no one.

A wise man will speak the truth and instruct others without harshness. Let us speak the truth with pleasant words that are healing to hear.

---

[680] Proverbs 10:12 (NKJV).
[681] Proverbs 16:18 (NASB).
[682] Proverbs 14:30 (NIV).
[683] Proverbs 16:23-24 (NIV).

Day 352

Solomon

The fear of the LORD leads to life: then one rests content, untouched by trouble.[684]

Two things I request of You (deprive me not before I die): remove falsehood and lies far from me; give me neither poverty nor riches—feed me with the food allotted to me; lest I be full and deny You, and say, "Who is the LORD?" Or lest I be poor and steal, and profane the name of my God.[685]

Buddha

[409] Him I call indeed a Brahmana who takes nothing in the world that is not given him, be it long or short, small or large, good or bad.

When we have too much, we can become prideful and complacent, and when we have too little, we can be plagued with worry, fear, and even resort to stealing. The Ten Commandments state, "You shall not steal."[686] Let us foster contentment regardless of our circumstances.

---

[684] Proverbs 19:23 (NIV).
[685] Proverbs 30:7-9 (NKJV). Proverbs 30 is attributed to Agur, son of Jakeh.
[686] Exodus 20:15 (NASB).

Day 353

Solomon

Buddha

The righteousness of the upright shall deliver them; but the treacherous shall be taken in their own iniquity.[687]

[410] Him I call indeed a Brahmana who fosters no desires for this world or for the next, has no inclinations, and is unshackled.

In seeking to live a righteous life, let us avoid being trapped and shackled by worldly desires.

Day 354

Solomon

Buddha

The mind of the prudent acquires knowledge, and the ear of the wise seeks knowledge.[688]

Buy the truth and do not sell it; get wisdom, discipline and understanding.[689]

[411] Him I call indeed a Brahmana who has no interests, and when he has understood (the truth), does not say How, how? and who has reached the depth of the Immortal.

The heart of the wise man seeks truth, wisdom and knowledge. Follow his example. Let us acquire them, keep them and not sell them. Let us search their depths.

---

[687] Proverbs 11:6 (ASV).
[688] Proverbs 18:15 (NASB).
[689] Proverbs 23:23 (NIV).

Day 355

Solomon	**Buddha**
Do not be wise in your own eyes; fear the LORD and shun evil.[690]	[412] Him I call indeed a Brahmana who in this world is above good and evil, above the bondage of both, free from grief, from sin, and from impurity.
A wise man is cautious and turns away from evil. . . .[691]	

Free from the bondage of evil, that is real freedom. Let us be wise in our choices and careful in our conduct to avoid doing evil.

---

[690] Proverbs 3:7 (NIV).
[691] Proverbs 14:16a (NASB).

Day 356

Solomon

Buddha

The LORD detests the thoughts of the wicked, but those of the pure are pleasing to him.[692]

But the path of the righteous is like the light of dawn, that shines brighter and brighter until the full day.[693]

[413] Him I call indeed a Brahmana who is bright like the moon, pure, serene, undisturbed, and in whom all gaiety is extinct.

Spotless and pure like a gleaming moon, may we have pure thoughts, hearts and hands. King David wrote,

> Who may ascend the hill of the LORD? Who may stand in his holy place? He who has clean hands and a pure heart, who does not lift up his soul to an idol or swear by what is false.[694]

---

[692] Proverbs 15:26 (NIV).
[693] Proverbs 4:18 (NASB).
[694] Psalm 24:3-4 (NIV), a psalm of King David, Solomon's father.

Day 357

Solomon	Buddha
Deceit is in the heart of those who devise evil, but counselors of peace have joy.[695]	[414] Him I call indeed a Brahmana who has traversed this miry road, the impassable world and its vanity, who has gone through, and reached the other shore, is thoughtful, guileless, free from doubts, free from attachment, and content.
The fear of the LORD leads to life: then one rests content, untouched by trouble.[696]	

The wise man is free from the practices of deceit and cheating of any kind. He is free from insidious, crafty cunning and planning in order to attain a selfish goal. He has passed through the world and all its vanity, to a peaceful, untroubled place of contentment. Let us throw off deceit and guile and be content.

---

[695] Proverbs 12:20 (NASB).
[696] Proverbs 19:23 (NIV).

Day 358

Solomon

Buddha

Happy is the man who finds wisdom, and the man who gains understanding; for her proceeds are better than the profits of silver, and her gain than fine gold. She is more precious than rubies, and all the things you may desire cannot compare with her.[697]

[415] Him I call indeed a Brahmana who in this world, leaving all desires, travels about without a home, and in whom all concupiscence is extinct.

Nothing we can desire is more valuable that wisdom. It will bring us a better return for our investment than silver or gold.

---

[697] Proverbs 3:13-15 (NKJV).

Day 359

Solomon

Buddha

A tranquil heart is life to the body, but passion is rottenness to the bones.[698]

He who loves money will not be satisfied with money, nor he who loves abundance with its income. This too is vanity. When good things increase, those who consume them increase. So what is the advantage to their owners except to look on? The sleep of the working man is pleasant, whether he eats little or much; but the full stomach of the rich man does not allow him to sleep.[699]

[416] Him I call indeed a Brahmana who, leaving all longings, travels about without a home, and in whom all covetousness is extinct.

It is unwise to desire for more, envy others, and covet what others have. These evils are insatiable. They will eat away at us until they eat our very bones.

---

[698] Proverbs 14:30 (NASB).
[699] Ecclesiastes 5:10-12 (NASB).

Day 360

Solomon

Buddha

The truly righteous man attains life, but he who pursues evil goes to his death. The LORD detests men of perverse heart but he delights in those whose ways are blameless. Be sure of this: the wicked will not go unpunished, but those who are righteous will go free.[700]

417 Him I call indeed a Brahmana who, after leaving all bondage to men, has risen above all bondage to the gods, and is free from all and every bondage.

The blameless, the pure, the truly righteous are free. Free from wickedness and free from evil desires. We ought to aspire to this freedom, leaving all bondage behind.

---

[700] Proverbs 11:19-21 (NIV).

Day 361

Solomon

Do not be overrighteous, neither be overwise—why destroy yourself? Do not be overwicked, and do not be a fool—why die before your time? It is good to grasp the one and not let go of the other. The man who fears God will avoid all extremes. Wisdom makes one wise man more powerful than ten rulers in a city.[701]

Buddha

[418] Him I call indeed a Brahmana who has left what gives pleasure and what gives pain, who is cold, and free from all germs (of renewed life), the hero who has conquered all the worlds.

Knowing we can leave behind evil desires and avoid extremes, this wisdom can renew us and help us to make the changes we need to in our lives.

---

[701] Ecclesiastes 7:16-19 (NIV).

Day 362

Solomon	Buddha
For the fate of the sons of men and the fate of beasts is the same. As one dies so dies the other; indeed, they all have the same breath and there is no advantage for man over beast, for all is vanity.[702]	[419] Him I call indeed a Brahmana who knows the destruction and the return of beings everywhere, who is free from bondage, welfaring (Sugata), and awakened (Buddha).
The righteousness of the upright delivers them, but the unfaithful are trapped by evil desires.[703]	[420] Him I call indeed a Brahmana whose path the gods do not know, nor spirits (Gandharvas), nor men, whose passions are extinct, and who is an Arhat (venerable).

Knowing we all will die ought to give us pause. In our limited time on this earth, may we extinguish evil desires and choose a righteous path.

---

[702] Ecclesiastes 3:19 (NASB).
[703] Proverbs 11:6 (NIV).

Day 363

Solomon

Buddha

Better is a little with
righteousness
than great income with
injustice.[704]

Incline my heart to Your
testimonies and not to
covetousness (robbery,
sensuality, unworthy
riches).[705]

[421] Him I call indeed a
Brahmana who calls nothing
his own, whether it be
before, behind, or between,
who is poor, and free from
the love of the world.

Let us be free from the love of the world. May we turn our hearts towards wisdom and away from covetousness and selfish gain. Jesus taught,

> Do not store up for yourselves treasures on earth, where moth and rust destroy, and where thieves break in and steal. But store up for yourselves treasures in heaven, where moth and rust do not destroy, and where thieves do not break in and steal. For where your treasure is, there your heart will be also. . . . No one can serve two masters. Either he will hate the one and love the other, or he will be devoted to the one and despise the other. You cannot serve both God and Money.[706]

---

[704] Proverbs 16:8 (NASB).
[705] Psalm 119:36 (AMP).
[706] Matthew 6:19-21, 24 (NIV).

And do not set your heart on what you will eat or drink; do not worry about it. For the pagan world runs after all such things, and your Father [in heaven] knows that you need them. . . . Sell your possessions and give to the poor. Provide purses for yourselves that will not wear out, a treasure in heaven that will not be exhausted, where no thief comes near and no moth destroys. For where your treasure is, there your heart will be also.[707]

---

[707] Luke 12:29-30, 33-34 (NIV).

Day 364

Solomon	Buddha

When the righteous triumph, there is great elation; but when the wicked rise to power, men go into hiding.[708]

[422] Him I call indeed a Brahmana, the manly, the noble, the hero, the great sage, the conqueror, the impassible, the accomplished, the awakened.

When we wash away all evil and conquer our passions, we are walking on the path of a righteous life. When we succeed and triumph, even those around us are joyful and elated. King David wrote,

> Commit your way to the LORD; trust in him and he will do this: He will make your righteousness shine like the dawn, the justice of your cause like the noonday sun.[709]

---

[708] Proverbs 28:12 (NIV).
[709] Psalm 37:5-6 (NIV), a psalm of King David, Solomon's father.

Day 365

Solomon

But the path of the just is like the shining sun, that shines ever brighter unto the perfect day.[710]

Buddha

[423] Him I call indeed a Brahmana who knows his former abodes, who sees heaven and hell, has reached the end of births, is perfect in knowledge, a sage, and whose perfections are all perfect.

For the just, reaching the end of their lives is like walking under the perfection of the bright shining sun. As we study and seek after wisdom and knowledge, let us walk a just path.

---

[710] Proverbs 4:18 (NKJV).

References

Friedrich Max Muller, trans., *The Dhammapada: A Collection of Verses, Being One of the Canonical Works of the Buddhists*, in vol. 10, Part 1, *The Sacred Books of the East*, translated by Various Oriental Scholars, edited by F. Max Muller, available at Dhammapada (Muller), Wikisource. This work is cited as "Dhammapada."

Scripture quotations marked (AMP) are taken from the *Amplified Bible*, Copyright © 1954, 1958, 1962, 1964, 1965, 1987 by The Lockman Foundation. Used by permission.

American Standard Version (ASV). Copyright © 1901 by Public Domain

Scripture quotations marked (KJV) are from the *King James Version*, which is in the public domain.

Scripture quotations marked (NASB) taken from the *New American Standard Bible®*, Copyright © 1960, 1962, 1963, 1968, 1971, 1972, 1973, 1975, 1977, 1995 by The Lockman Foundation. Used by permission.

Scripture quotations marked (NIV) are taken from the HOLY BIBLE, NEW INTERNATIONAL VERSION®. NIV® Copyright ©1973, 1978, 1984 by International Bible Society. Used by permission of Zondervan. All rights reserved.

Scripture quotations marked (NKJV) are taken from the *New King James Version®*. Copyright © 1982 by Thomas Nelson, Inc. Used by permission. All rights reserved.

For formatting purposes, the line breaks in quotations have not been retained.